Transforming
Central Government

Public Policy and Management

Series Editor: Professor R.A.W. Rhodes, Department of Politics, University of York.
Series Advisers: Professor Peter Jackson, University of Leicester and Professor Mike Connolly, University of Ulster.

The effectiveness of public policies is a matter of public concern and the efficiency with which policies are put into practice is a continuing problem for governments of all political persuasions. This series contributes to these debates by publishing informed, in-depth and contemporary analyses of public administration, public policy and public management.

The intention is to go beyond the usual textbook approach to the analysis of public policy and management and to encourage authors to move debate about their issue forward. In this sense, each book both describes current thinking and research, and explores future policy directions. Accessibility is a key feature and, as a result, the series will appeal to academics and their students as well as to the informed practitioner.

Current Titles Include:

Whose Utility? The Social Impact of Public Utility Privatization and Regulation in Britain
John Ernst

Transforming Central Government: The Next Steps Initiative
Patricia Greer

Implementing Thatcherite Policies: Audit of an Era
David Marsh and R.A.W. Rhodes (eds)

British Aid and International Trade
O. Morrissey, B. Smith and E. Horesh

Markets and Managers: New Issues in the Delivery of Welfare
Peter Taylor-Gooby and Robyn Lawson (eds)

Social Care in a Mixed Economy
Gerald Wistow, Martin Knapp, Brian Hardy and Caroline Allen

New Managerialism: Administrative Reform in Whitehall and Canberra
Spencer Michael Zifcak

Transforming Central Government

The Next Steps Initiative

Patricia Greer

Open University Press
Buckingham · Philadelphia

Open University Press
Celtic Court
22 Ballmoor
Buckingham
MK18 1XW

and
1900 Frost Road, Suite 101
Bristol, PA 19007, USA

First Published 1994

A catalogue record of this book is available from the British Library

ISBN 0 335 19114 2 (pbk)   0 335 19115 0 (hbk)

Library of Congress Cataloging-in-Publication Data

Greer, Patricia, 1963–
    Transforming central government: the Next Steps initiative/by
Patricia Greer.
        p.   cm.
    Includes bibliographical references and index.
    ISBN 0–335–19115–0. – ISBN 0–335–19114–2 (pbk)
    1. Administrative agencies–Great Britain–Reorganization.
2. Great Britain–Politics and government–1979–   3. Civil service
reform–Great Britain.   4. Great Britain. Dept. of Social Security.
I. Title
JN425.G76 1994
354.4107'7–dc20   93–38386
                                                                    CIP

Typeset by Inforum, Rowlands Castle, Hants
Printed in Great Britain by St Edmundsbury Press, Bury St Edmunds, Suffolk

Contents

Introduction

This book is about the Next Steps initiative, the initiative which is currently transforming the British system of government. Next Steps was launched in 1988 with a report from the Prime Minister's Efficiency Unit.[1] The main aims of the initiative are to create durable improvements in management in government and to deliver services more efficiently and effectively within available resources for the benefit of customers, taxpayers and staff. One of the most distinguishing features of Next Steps is the structural change of creating executive agencies from the operational arms of government. By 5 April 1993, 89 agencies had been established. Over 260,000 civil servants are working in agencies; this represents some 45 per cent of total civil servants. In addition, 19 further agency candidates have been announced covering over 25,000 more civil servants which will take the proportion of civil servants working in agencies to nearly 50 per cent. The aim is to have over 90 per cent of civil servants working in agencies by the end of 1995. Next Steps has implications for the nature, content and skills of civil servants' jobs and for the organizational structures in which they operate but more importantly, Next Steps has much wider implications for the future of the civil service and for its constitutional role as the Executive.

In addition, Next Steps now has two important relatives which form a part of the package of current reforms – the Citizen's Charter and the Competing for Quality (Market Testing) initiative. The Citizen's Charter was launched in July 1991 and aims to improve public services in order to respond better to the needs and wishes of customers and users, and to find more effective and efficient ways of organizing and delivering public services.[2] In central government the effect of the Citizen's Charter has been to put more pressure on departments and agencies to prioritize their aim of bringing new and improved services to customers. The Competing for Quality initiative also acts to prioritize and direct the development of Next Steps. The Competing for Quality white paper was published in November 1991 and sets out proposals requiring departments and agencies to open up many of their functions to competition from private sector or other public sector contractors.[3] In other words, the Competing for Quality initiative is about departments and agencies tendering for bids from contractors to run many of their functions.

Next Steps addresses the age old problem of how to run government. There is nothing new in the dilemmas raised by Next Steps. How do we divide policy and operational matters? How do we balance accountability and autonomy? How do we minimize transaction costs? These issues were raised in earlier moves to arm's length government. Other features of Next Steps are also familiar from other areas of public policy. One of the main features of Next Steps is the development of contracts to manage operational activities to be carried out either by the public sector or increasingly, particularly as the Competing for Quality initiative matures, by the private sector. Next Steps is about the move to management *by* contract and the management *of* contracts. There are parallels with these developments and the current move to develop quasi-markets in many areas of public sector service delivery including health, the personal social services and education.

In many ways the Next Steps solution is, as its name suggests, the next step in a programme of central government reforms. However, it combines this incremental 'next stepping' with a new emphasis on business ideas and language. Many of the characteristics of Next Steps are old friends in new clothes. What is new about Next Steps is the particular combination of features coming together at the present time and the prevailing climate of belief that the public sector must learn from the private sector and indeed that the boundaries of the public and private sectors should shift. Britain is not unique in its present thinking and language about how to run central government. Other western democracies are also embracing similar language and thinking but there are some important differences in how these ideas are being translated into practice.

The aim of this book is therefore to use the case study of the Department of Social Security and its agencies to examine the development of Next Steps and to consider the implications of the Next Steps experiment for Whitehall, for the British system of government, for other countries involved in the decentralization of activity and for administrative theory. The case study of the Department of Social Security provides a detailed examination of the experiences of one department whilst also raising issues of wider relevance. The Department of Social Security is particularly suitable for this kind of exercise because its agencies represent most 'types' of new arrangements.

The book is founded on material generated by a three year study funded by the Leverhulme Trust. The study was based on documentary analysis and interviews conducted on lobby terms with some of the main players in the Next Steps arena: ministers, parliamentarians, Department of Social Security senior officials, senior Treasury and Office of the Minister for the Civil Service (now Office of Public Service and Science) officials, agency chief executives and senior agency officials, select committee officials, National Audit Office directors and senior Canadian and New Zealand public servants. The text attributes beliefs, ideas and quotations to the appropriate people wherever possible but does not attribute where this may cause embarrassment to the individual concerned.

Chapters 1 and 2 set out the wider issues and put the initiative into a historical and theoretical context. Chapter 1 outlines the similarities and differences in the features and the theoretical concerns raised by Next Steps and by earlier initiatives. It then considers how administrative theory can help to explain other features of Next Steps and can help us to analyse its progress. Chapter 2 asks what is so different about Next Steps to make it revolutionary rather than evolutionary and why it should come now.

Chapters 3 to 6 analyse the process of developing Next Steps drawing on the case study of the Department of Social Security and its agencies. Chapter 3 introduces the Department of Social Security and its agencies. It outlines how the department's agencies range across the spectrum of agency types and therefore raise issues of wider relevance and it identifies other features which may affect the development of agencies. Chapter 4 introduces the main organizational actors involved with Next Steps, outlines their positions in the Next Steps arena and examines the changing roles and relationships between these bodies in shaping the development of Next Steps. Chapter 5 focuses on the move to 'contract government'. It examines the processes of developing the contracts, the content of the contracts and evaluates their success in allowing greater autonomy within a framework of accountability. Chapter 6 again draws on the main themes of accountability versus autonomy and the distinction between policy and operational issues in examining the effect of Next Steps on parliamentary accountability.

Chapters 7 to 9 evaluate the effect of Next Steps. Chapter 7 examines the fundamental changes to the organization, size and culture of the civil service and the wider implications of these changes for the future of the civil service and for its constitutional role. Chapter 8 draws on interviews conducted in two countries based on the Westminster model, New Zealand and Canada, to ask whether Next Steps is a British eccentricity or whether it is a part of something more general. Chapter 9 provides an overall evaluation of the success of Next Steps in achieving its aims of improving efficiency and quality of service and from the point of view of customers, staff and parliamentarians. It also asks whether Next Steps has outlined useful lessons either for future British reforms or for those of other countries and whether it has been a success in terms of its contribution to administrative theory.

I am indebted to the many people who made this book possible. I wish to thank the many officials in Britain, Canada and New Zealand who by convention must remain nameless but who were most generous with their valuable time and insights. I also wish to thank the Leverhulme Trust for funding the research. My particular thanks goes to Rudolf Klein for talking me into employment as a researcher at Bath and for reading and providing productive comments on draft chapters. Finally, my personal thanks goes to all who kept me relatively sane throughout the project – my friends and colleagues and my horses, Shiraz and Octavius.

Notes

1 Efficiency Unit (1988) *Improving Management in Government: The Next Steps*. London, HMSO.
2 *The Citizen's Charter: Raising the Standard* (1991) Cm 1599. London, HMSO.
3 HM Treasury (1991) *Competing for Quality*, Cm 1730. London, HMSO.

1

Next Steps: Origins

The ideas of economists and political philosophers, both when they are right and when they are wrong, are more powerful than is commonly understood. Indeed, the world is ruled by little else . . . Madmen in authority, who hear voices in the air, are distilling their frenzy from some academic scribbler a few years back.

(Keynes)[1]

Next Steps aims to precipitate action, not thought or debate. It claims to be a pragmatic initiative rooted in action rather than in history or in theory and yet neither the features of Next Steps nor the issues they raise are new. Despite this claim this chapter shows that Next Steps is, albeit unconsciously, rooted in both history and theory. Many of the characteristics of Next Steps are old friends in new clothes. There is nothing new about arm's length government, the emphasis on a more specialist civil service, the shift in emphasis from policy to management, the focus on efficiency and costs of service delivery, the emphasis on performance measurement or the shift in emphasis from inputs and process to outputs.

Similarly, there is very little that is new about the questions and dilemmas raised by Next Steps. Next Steps addresses the age old problems of how to run government. How do we make the public service more efficient and effective when there is no profit motive? How do we ensure that managers have sufficient autonomy to get on with the job whilst ensuring that those managers are accountable for their actions? How do we allow public servants autonomy when ministers are ultimately accountable for what those public servants do? What is the appropriate relationship between a minister and his or her departmental advisers and the operational arms of a department? How do we distinguish between policy and operational issues? The issues have been repeatedly raised with past attempts to reform government and have been comprehensively addressed by administrative theory.

The aim of this chapter is therefore to consider the Efficiency Unit report which launched Next Steps and to outline what Next Steps has drawn and learnt from earlier practical and theoretical attempts to reform government. The chapter then considers what theory can tell us about the future development of Next Steps.

The Efficiency Unit report

The report launching the initiative from the Prime Minister's Efficiency Unit, 'Improving Management in Government: The Next Steps', is more like a report from a management consultancy firm than a traditional civil service review. It is glossy, bold and evangelical. The traditional mandarin style of drafting to avoid commitment has been replaced by a fresh passion for revitalization and change. The style and thrust of the report reflects the views and skills of its relatively youthful authors. The Next Steps report was written by a new breed of civil servant. It is predicated on the belief that there is an important discipline of 'management' which has been traditionally and mistakenly overlooked by the civil service in favour of traditional 'policy skills'.

Next Steps professes to be all about 'improving management in government'. The aims are 'to leave managers free to manage', 'to ensure that senior managers have experience of the skills and practical reality of management', for departments 'to develop specialised management skills'. The expectation is that improving management is the key to improving overall organizational performance.

Fulton

This belief in management is not new. Over 20 years ago the Fulton committee, set up by a Labour Government, also saw management as a key issue in civil service reform; they identified two definitions of 'management'. The first was an all embracing definition:

> Management, as we understand it, consists of the formulation and operation of the policy of the enterprise. This can be seen as a continuum ranging from first line supervision through a hierarchy of line managers to the board of directors. At each level assets – whether human, financial or material – have to be deployed in the manner best calculated to achieve particular objectives which contribute to the overall policy objectives formulated by the board.[2]

The second definition devised by the committee took account of the added 'political' dimension to the work of the civil service which manifests itself in public accountability and ultimate political direction. Within this context, the committee distinguished four aspects which make up the total management task of the civil service:

- formulation of a policy under political direction;
- creating the 'machinery' for implementation of policy;

- operation of the administrative machine;
- accountability to Parliament and the public.[3]

The Fulton committee identified some important differences between the managerial environments of the civil service and of industry and commerce. One major difference the committee identified was that in big firms top management are primarily concerned with the evaluation of different courses of action based on research whereas in the civil service, top management is largely preoccupied with reacting to such immediate pressures as ministers' cases, parliamentary debates and questions, reports of parliamentary committees and deputations.[4] Despite these major differences the Fulton committee concluded that management in the civil service has much in common with management in industry:

> Both are concerned with the formulation of policy and its implementation. Though most of the Civil Service cannot qualify its performance in terms of the financial return on resources, both it and industry are concerned with meeting objectives at the lowest possible cost. They are both concerned with making the best use of the scarce resources of skilled manpower for which they compete.[5]

The planting of these ideas as seeds over 20 years ago has paved the way for them now to be harvested. It is however interesting to note how the assumptions have changed in what civil service costs can and should be measured. Like Next Steps, Fulton emphasized the importance of knowing the unit costs of services and functions but, as the above extract illustrates, assumed that the extent to which this mode of performance measurement was limited because of the very nature of the civil service.

Public good: Private bad

A related assumption which underpins the Next Steps report is that the private sector is more efficient and effective than the public sector. Next Steps promotes the idea that public sector managers have much to learn from their private sector counterparts. Accordingly, many of the private sector management techniques and much of the private sector language is increasingly being adopted to become common parlance within the civil service.

Again, the foundations for this assumption lie in the history of public administration. The Fulton report also declared that the public sector had much to learn from the private sector and that the ideas and techniques are transferable.

The 'amateur generalist' versus a 'specialist' civil service

The Next Steps emphasis on creating a more specialist and focused civil service which promotes 'directed training and career development' is also not new.

This push to training people for particular areas of work rather than providing them with generalist civil service training again has the familiar tone of the Fulton report. Fulton recommended a break from the 'amateur generalist'. The committee found that generalist administrators tended to lack expertise in any particular area, and that this consequently inhibited effective policy making, prevented fundamental policy evaluation, and led to inadequate relationships with outside organizations. The Fulton committee therefore recommended an integration of the grading structure for specialists and generalists and more training for specialists in management. The committee also recommended more flexibility and movement in and out of the civil service.

Clearly the diagnosis is similar to that of Next Steps even if there are some differences in the recommended cures. The recommendation of more movement in and out of the public service clearly fits with the Next Steps notion of short term contracts.

So, it seems that the authors of the Next Steps report who began their careers in the post Fulton environment carried with them a number of assumptions which directed the report's style, content and recommendations. These assumptions are founded in Fulton but are now possibly more powerful as they are being raised in an environment where the ideas have become familiar to rising administrators and possibly therefore more palatable.

The new public management

The evangelical style of the Next Steps report suggests that it is a document independent of history or theory. The very *raison d'être* of the report was the fact that earlier initiatives had not been successful in achieving all their aims. Next Steps is, as its name suggests, the latest step in a line of reforms which have been variously labelled but which have come to be commonly known as the 'new public management'.[6] The features of the new public management has been broadly categorized by Aucoin, Hood, Hood and Jackson[6] and others as featuring:

- a shift to disaggregation in public service organization;
- a preference for limited term contract employment of senior staff over traditional career tenure; wholly monetized incentives rather than the traditional structure of control in the public sector through a mix of non-monetary factors (ethos, status, culture) and uniform fixed salaries; top managerial 'freedom to manage' over a network of constraints (notably by central personnel agencies) on action by line management;
- a divorce of provision from production (or delivery) in public service;
- an emphasis on cost cutting;
- a shift from policy to management with the focus primarily on efficiency and costs of service delivery – leading to an emphasis on quantifiable methods of performance and investment appraisal and efficiency criteria;
- a shift from process to outputs in controls and accountability mechanisms.[7]

The Financial Management Initiative, Rayner and MINIS

The immediate predecessor to Next Steps was the financial management initiative (FMI), launched in May 1982. But once more the FMI was an incremental step building on work which was already underway in individual departments. Next Steps would not have been a possible goal within the British traditions of parliamentary accountability without a certain degree of sophistication in information systems and performance reporting. The backbones of the required structures were mainly established by the series of reforms which spanned the 1970s and 1980s.

The Rayner scrutinies involved small teams focusing on particular aspects of their departments' work and reviewing whether it is being conducted in the most cost efficient manner. Departments also developed arrangements for providing ministers and top officials with better information. One such system was Michael Heseltine's Management Information Systems for Ministers (MINIS) which was developed first in the Department of Environment since 1979 and was then adopted by the Ministry of Defence. The aim of MINIS was to inform ministers and top management of activities, costs and performance within individual management areas. The aim was also that departmental managers would derive the information necessary to do their jobs from MINIS.

The aim of the financial management initiative was to develop these individual department initiatives and to promote in each department an organization and a system in which managers at all levels would have:

1 a clear view of their objectives; and means to assess, and wherever possible measure, outputs or performance in relation to those objectives;
2 well-defined responsibility for making the best use of their resources, including a critical scrutiny of output and value for money; and
3 the information (particularly about costs), the training and the access to expert advice that they needed to exercise their responsibilities effectively.[8]

The Financial Management Initiative did not entirely succeed in achieving these aims. Indeed, departments' progress in implementing the initiative was examined and criticized by the Committee of Public Accounts of Session 1986–87. The committee concluded that a major effort was needed to speed up implementation and emphasized the need for clear and preferably quantified objectives in all areas, with yardsticks against which to measure performance; and that high priority should be given to examining how line managers could be delegated more effective responsibility for the resources they controlled, including more flexibility on staffing matters.[9] In other words, the committee was stressing the need for a 'Next Steps'.

The Financial Management Initiative did however establish the cornerstones for Next Steps. It succeeded in ensuring that departments were more aware of the importance of cost consciousness and performance measurement. It also resulted in the development of a prolific number of performance measures and in departmental management and financial management information systems. This regime of cost consciousness and reporting provided the base on which the notion of 'management by contract' could be constructed. The idea of contracting agencies and, in particular, key agency staff, to achieve certain ends within specified resources would not have been possible without the faith of central departments in existing and future tools for measuring and reporting agency performance. Chapter 5 outlines how and why these tools have been undergoing extensive review and refinement but what is important here is that it is the *evolution* of these tools which has resulted in one of the most radical elements of Next Steps.

The structural change

Again, one of the most distinguishing features of Next Steps, the structural reform of creating semi-autonomous agencies from the operational arms of government, is not unprecedented. The issues are also familiar. How do we achieve the balance of ensuring that the arm's length agency has sufficient autonomy to perform its task effectively whilst ensuring that the agency remains accountable for their actions to central departments, to ministers and possibly directly to Parliament? How do we decide on the appropriate division of responsibilities between the agency and central departments? What is the appropriate role of the agency in 'policy' issues, and how far should ministers and central departments become involved in the day to day operations of the agency? How do we draw the line between these 'policy' and 'operational' issues? In this respect Next Steps is again an incremental step developing earlier forms of arm's length arrangements.

These issues have consistently arisen throughout the history of arm's length government whose origins stem back to the origins of government. Arm's length government covers a whole spectrum of arrangements from central legislation with local administration to central legislation with legislation and administration by a private body.

Balancing local autonomy and central control in the case of social security

Social security provides a continuing example of attempts to balance autonomy and control which have continued from the time of the Poor Law right through to the present day. The Poor Law Act of 1601 laid the foundations for a system of poor law relief administered within each parish by people appointed by magistrates. The failure of the centre to regulate the local relief resulted in vast differences in the ways in which the local schemes were being administered and in the relief available. The Poor Law Commission, appointed in 1832 to review the existing system of relief, concluded that local discretion had opened the way to corruption, intimidation and inconsistency. The report therefore recommended a central board to administer to the Poor Law with powers to control local practices. The board was attempting to reassert uniformity to existing practices through tightening up the existing arrangements for arm's length control – equipping local parishes with the legislation and letting them get on with it.

Similar difficulties of controlling local discretion whilst allowing sufficient autonomy to meet local and individual needs have continued to emerge within our modern social security system. An example is the appropriate method for making payments to people on benefits to meet exceptional needs which they are unable to meet out of their weekly benefit payments such as for cookers, baby items or furniture. Before 1980 the solution was to allow local office staff considerable discretion to make such payments within a limited set of guide-lines. The incidence and costs of these payments rose considerably and in 1980 attempts were made to minimize local office staff discretion. The result was a long set of regulations controlling the circumstances under which these exceptional needs payments must be awarded. The number of payments was reduced at first but then rose as claimants, welfare rights workers and staff learnt their way around these regulations. A further attempt to impose arm's length control on this area came with the introduction of the Social Fund in 1988. Under the Social Fund, local offices have annual cash limits on the amounts they can pay in these special needs payments and in most cases the payments are now loans, that is, recipients must repay any loans out of their weekly benefits. Evidence is emerging that again, there are considerable differences in practices between local offices but the Social Fund has also been criticized for being too inflexible to meet individual needs!

Balancing autonomy and control in the British corporations, nationalized industries and non-departmental public bodies

Further down the spectrum of arm's length government and possibly closer to the case of executive agencies fall the British corporations such as the BBC and Imperial Airways which were created in the 1920s. Then there are the nationalized industries such as the National Coal Board and the Post Office which were acquired mainly from the private sector to operate as trading corporations under the command of government. Third, there are the non-departmental public bodies (NDPBs). The Cabinet Office and Treasury Guide to departments on NDPBs defines them as: 'a body which has a role in the processes of national government, but is not a government department, and accordingly operates to a greater or lesser extent at arm's length from Ministers.'[10] The guide then goes on to distinguish three categories of NDPB:

1 bodies with executive, administrative, regulatory or commercial functions;
2 advisory committees and commissions;
3 tribunals and other judicial bodies.

Whatever the type of body or the category of NDPB, once again the issues have that familiar ring. How do you allow the necessary freedoms and at the same time ensure that these bodies remain accountable both to Parliament and to the public? How do you ensure continued ministerial control? How do you separate the responsibilities for 'policy' and 'operations' between the body and its guardian department and/or minister? The Select Committee on Nationalized Industries reported on ministerial control in the Nationalized Industries in 1968 finding that:

> What is worrying is the recurring revelation in the Committee evidence of confusion between Chairmen and Ministers about the nature and purposes of the government's policies, about how policies should be prepared and, in particular, about the purposes and desirable methods of Ministerial control itself . . . An industry's programme is considered, to some degree or another, by the Department, by the Department of Exchequer and Audit [now National Audit Office] and by the Treasury. But what their respective contributions are – or are meant to be – appears to be far from clear . . .[11]

Similarly on the issue of departmental bodies the Pliatzky report stated:

> It is clearly not always easy to get the right balance between dis-engagement from detail and reserved powers of supervision or interven-tion, while great care has to be taken if the objective in principle of creating an accountable unit of management is not to be frustrated by the difficulties in practice in making effective arrangements to secure ac-countability for performance.[12]

The committee went on to conclude that there are both advantages and disadvantages in hiving off activities to arm's length from government and that in view of this 'we should not think in terms of a further considerable extension of "hiving off" . . . as an instrument for securing improved efficiency and economy across a wide range of public activities'.

This recommendation came 12 years after the 1968 Fulton report which had called for an examination of the possibility of a considerable extension of 'hiving off' especially in areas where government is in the business of providing a service or services to the public – to areas closer to the core of government. The Fulton committee had reported:

> It has been put to us that accountable management is most effectively introduced when an activity is separately established outside any govern-ment department, and that this solution should be adopted for many executive activities, especially the provision of services to the community.[13]

So why the divergence in opinion between the Fulton and Pliatzky commit-tees? And why, in view of the similarities in the findings of the Pliatzky committee and the Select Committee on Nationalized Industries, should Next Steps be pursuing the Fulton recommendation of extending the 'hiving off' of government functions?

This is partly explained by the fact that Next Steps does differ from earlier attempts at arm's length government in some important ways. Next Steps has learnt from these earlier experiences and has sought solutions to the dilemmas by, albeit unconsciously, drawing on theory. Next Steps has learnt that there must be clearer divisions of responsibility and accountability than have been evident in earlier experiences of arm's length government and has looked to administrative theory in its attempt to avoid the ambiguity, uncertainty and distortion which resulted from earlier arm's length arrangements.

The move to contract government

The solution which Next Steps has adopted in its attempt to resolve the age old problems of arm's length government – of balancing autonomy and accountability and of clearly distinguishing between the appropriate responsibilities of the various actors – is to regulate relationships and responsibilities through the use of contracts. Next Steps is about creating a series of clearly specified client/contractor relationships. This step is again not entirely new. Contract government is now well ingrained into the culture of many areas of public sector service delivery including health, personal social services, education, housing and a number of local government services such as refuse collection.

At the most basic level agencies have framework documents which, along with the annual business plans and the five yearly corporate plans, establish the framework in which agencies must operate. For example, amongst other things, the framework documents aim to define the respective roles of the various players; ministers, the Treasury, departments and agencies. Chief executives and agency key designated staff are also individually contracted to meet with business plan specifications and have sizeable proportions of their pay contingent on their success. At a more detailed level, agencies contract agencies through service level agreements to perform certain functions. In other words, the 'contractor' becomes a client which must manage its dealings with other 'contractor' agencies.

Again following other areas of public policy delivery, Next Steps and its related Competing for Quality initiative have taken this move to management *by* contract one step further. Increasingly the move is also to management *of* contract as more of agency responsibilities are contracted out to the private sector. This move to 'contract' government as a solution to earlier difficulties with ambiguities in responsibilities and relationships draws directly from a branch of micro economics – agency theory.

Agency theory

Agency theory is basically the study of exchanges between two parties called the principal and the agent in situations where pure market organization does not apply.[14] It is based on the proposition that social and political life can be understood as a series of 'contracts' in which one party, referred to as the principal, enters into exchanges with another party, referred to as the agent.[15]

Agency theory assumes that individuals are out to pursue their self interests possibly at the expense of the interests of others. The assumption is that the interests of principals and agents are likely to conflict. The important issue in agency theory is therefore how principals are to control agents and to ensure that the agents' self interest is in meeting the principals' objectives. Agency theory sees that objectives must be clarified and agreed and that both/all parties should be held accountable for the achievement of those objectives.

Next Steps goes down this contractual path as a means of ensuring that 'agents' act in the interests of their 'principals'. These contracts, with their performance measures and targets, also allow the 'principals' to monitor the activities of 'agents' in meeting the required ends. The operational arms of government will enter into a number of contractual relations in which they may be acting as both principals and agents. For example, an agency may be the agent of its parent department and also the principal in agreements with other bodies who are contracted to produce goods or services for the agency.

As an aside, a point that is worth mentioning here but to which we return in detail in Chapter 4 is the degree of ambiguity in the Next Steps arrangements about precisely who is the principal and who is the agent. Taking as an example the agency business plans, are they contracts between parent departments and agencies? Ministers and agencies? Treasury and agencies? The Office of Public Service and Science and agencies? Are chief executives' contracts between themselves and the permanent secretary? Themselves and their minister? No matter how tightly defined the contracts, this ambiguity will clearly lead to some confusion over respective responsibilities.

The issue of a controlling b is complicated by the what agency theorists have termed 'asymmetric information'. This situation occurs where for one reason or another the principal is unable to observe the actions of the agent and the agent has more information on what he or she plans and is doing than he or she may wish to tell the principal. This difficulty was identified by Spremann who saw that 'the agent could make any promise with respect to his action and depart from it later on just because the principal is unable to control or to monitor the agent's decision making'.[16]

Heymann identifies a number of ways in which principals can try to ensure that agents' interests and actions are aligned with their own interests. They can use various kinds of incentives and sanctions to align the agents' interests to their own; they can closely monitor the behaviour of the agent; or they can enter into a bonding arrangement whereby the agent gives a guarantee to act in line with the principals' interests or provide compensation if the contract is breached.[17]

In line with this theory Next Steps encourages the development of control mechanisms to ensure the alignment of interests. The sanctions for agencies not meeting their targets or fulfilling the principals' interests include possible dismissal for agency chief executives who are appointed on short term contracts and the withholding of group performance pay (which may be paid to all agency staff if the annual targets are met) and of individual performance related pay, in particular to senior agency staff for whom the sums in question can be up to 12 per cent of salary.

Public choice theory

The related strand of micro economic theory on which Next Steps draws (although again possibly unconsciously) is public choice theory. Public choice theory is epitomized by the work of Niskanen (1971, 1973), Downs (1957, 1967) and Tullock (1965).[18] It is essentially an American based school of thought with three main strands which evolved in three different areas.[19] The development of public choice theory marked the beginnings of the application of the discipline of economics to aspects of everyday life. The application of public choice theory to bureaucracies added a totally new dimension to existing theories on the nature of bureaucracies.

The term 'bureaucracy' and the study of bureaucracy originated in France in the late eighteenth century.[20] From this time Max Weber's work described and evaluated the structures and main features of bureaucracies. Weber's basic premiss was that bureaucracy is a good thing. He saw bureaucratic organization as technically superior to any other form of organization. Essentially he saw that in every bureaucracy there are formal and informal goals, hierarchies and communications networks and that these all work towards the achievement of the organization's formal goals.

By contrast, the application of economics to the study of bureaucracy by those who have come to be known as the public choice theorists, began with the premiss that all individuals are self interested and will pursue their own goals. This is summarized by Mueller who states that 'The basic behavioural postulate of public choice, as for economics, is that man is an egoistic, rational, utility maximiser.'[21] The essential theory is that the self interest of bureaucrats has resulted in a distortion of the 'market' of supply and demand of public goods and services.

Most of the attention of public choice writers has been on the supply curve, as shown in Figure 1.1. The argument is that bureaux maximize their budgets but because they are, to a certain extent, limited by demand in the extent to which they can increase supply, the result of any increase in budgets is that unit costs of goods or services increase. On the issue of demand public choice theorists are divided; most public choice theorists assume that the government is prepared to pay for more bureau services than the electorate would choose if they could buy them themselves.[22] By contrast, Downs argues that governments under supply public goods and services because they achieve more kudos from the electorate by pandering to the wishes of special interest groups.[23] For the purposes of this chapter what is important is that the public choice premiss of self interested bureaucrats increasing their budgets and distorting an efficient market is the rationale behind Next Steps.

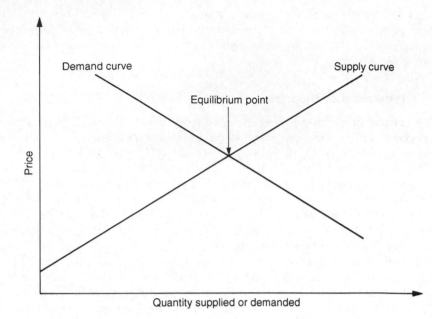

Demand curve

Supply curve

Equilibrium point

Price

Quantity supplied or demanded

Figure 1.1   Supply and demand curve

Next Steps is being introduced by a government with the aim of reducing the role and size of the civil service. Next Steps develops the concept of a 'market' for executive goods and services and questions its monopoly over certain parts of this market. In essence and in public choice/economists terminology, Next Steps is aiming to move supply back to the point of equilibrium and to ensure that the unit costs of supplying goods and services are not artificially inflated by bureaucrats' self interest.

Next Steps is adopting a series of strategies in attempting to create this efficient market. The first of these is directly lifted from the public choice school which states that one way of controlling bureaucratic self interest is to separate advisory, regulatory and delivery functions which, it says, should be undertaken by different agencies and wherever possible, contracted out. One of the most distinguishing features of Next Steps is its move to separate advisory, regulatory and delivery functions. Executive agencies are being established to perform the administrative and regulatory functions of government at arm's length from government.

This separation of functions has become practicable with the development of technology. The notion of central departments controlling agencies from arm's length whilst remaining ultimately accountable for their actions requires good management and financial information systems.

Further strategies to ensure the re-establishment of an efficient market for public goods and services include the introduction of competition between the public and private sectors for some executive functions and the contracting out to the private sector of some of these functions (even where this may not be immediately justifiable in terms of value for money). In addition, Next Steps introduction of group pay bonuses, individual performance related pay and the increased freedoms for agency staff are all grounded in public choice theory which advocates 'buying' self interest through the provision of such incentives.[24]

Contrary to popular belief, it seems that Keynes was right about his academic scribblers; Next Steps is, albeit unconsciously, grounded in history and in theory. The ideas behind Next Steps, albeit unconsciously, clearly draw on micro economics' agency and public choice theories. Next Steps is also not the first initiative to apply these micro economic theories to government. The reforms over the last 25 years are also, albeit to a lesser extent, fundamentally grounded in public choice and agency theory and have paved the way for Next Steps by developing the tools and structures required for it and by making the environment more amenable to change. However, the fact that earlier theories tell us where many of Next Steps ideas come from is interesting but probably not very useful. Theory is most useful when it informs us about the future and an increasingly popular branch of agency theory, transaction cost analysis, does precisely that: it informs us about the future development of Next Steps.

Transaction costs analysis

Transaction costs analysis focuses on the costs involved in principals' contracting to and monitoring and controlling agents.[25] This body of literature reveals some of the costs involved in establishing executive agencies and also tells us about the future costs of executive agencies. In turn, Next Steps adds a new dimension to the existing literature on transaction costs.

Transaction costs analysis was originally developed to explain the growth of large firms in capitalist society.[26] Oliver Williamson saw transaction costs as the costs of a principal controlling and monitoring an agent and ensuring that the agent fulfils the formal goals of the principal. Williamson's premiss was that firms will aim to minimize their transaction costs and that when certain conditions prevail and contract costs are high, firms integrate either vertically, that is, merge with their supplier and/or purchaser, or horizontally, that is, merge with similar companies competing in the same markets.

Next Steps establishes executive agencies which are to be controlled at arm's length from government and Williamson's analysis highlights that this structural change will inevitably involve additional transaction costs. There are three types of costs involved in establishing and running executive agencies. There are the initial costs of establishing the agencies, the recurring costs of revising structures and frameworks and the additional running costs incurred for example, in monitoring and controlling the agencies. The experience of Next Steps shows that there are three groups of transaction costs:

1 transitional transaction costs,
2 periodic transaction costs,
3 permanent transaction costs.

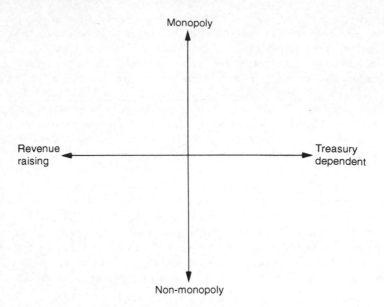

Figure 1.2   Typology of agencies

Transitional transaction costs are the costs of setting up the agency – for example, the costs of establishing the necessary financial and management information systems, the costs of consultants advising on issues such as personnel structures and arrangements, the costs of relocating functions. Periodic transaction costs are recurring costs such as developing and revising framework documents, business and corporate plans. The permanent transaction costs are the ongoing costs of delegating certain responsibilities to agencies and possibly forfeiting the benefits of economies of scale, for example, in carrying out personnel and finance work centrally rather than in each agency and in departmental headquarters. This revelation that different time periods incur different types of transaction costs adds a new dimension to the existing body of transaction costs theory.

The conditions which Williamson identified as increasing contract costs are:

uncertainty – the inability to foresee or control environmental changes;
small numbers bargaining – when there are few players for contracts;
asset specificity – when specific skills are required which may be difficult to replace from elsewhere;
bounded rationality – where individuals have limited information or cognitive capacity;
opportunism – where officials have the tendency to pursue their own interests.

One of the key determinants of an agency's development must be the nature of its business and whether or not it raises money from its services or products.

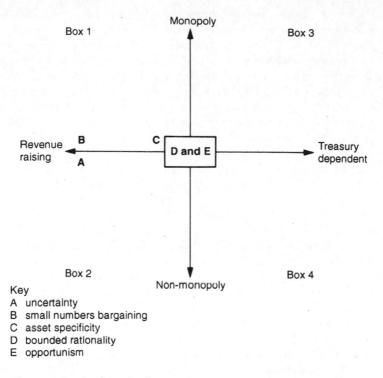

Figure 1.3   Applying Williamson's categories to the typology of agencies

Clearly those agencies raising revenue from receipts and competing for the 'markets' have more scope to develop as autonomous arms of government than those agencies which are entirely dependent on vote funding and provide a monopoly service close to the core of government. Figure 1.2 outlines a model for thinking about the different types of agencies and their potential for development. Using this typology we can consider the extent to which the Williamson conditions apply to each of the agency 'types'.

Figure 1.3 shows that the conditions which Williamson identifies as increasing contracting costs are present primarily in those agencies most likely to develop furthest as autonomous business enterprises, perhaps to the extent of full privatization.

First, there is greater uncertainty in contracts with those agencies who are revenue raising non-monopolies. Examples of such agencies include the Central Office of Information, the Civil Service College, the Queen Elizabeth II Conference Centre Executive Agency and the Department of Social Security's Information Technology Services Agency. These agencies operate in more uncertain markets than any of the other types of agencies in that they are less likely to know what future demand for their services will be. In addition, these agencies are facing increasingly uncertain future markets as they are now having to compete for much of their work with the private sector. As an aside, these agencies are themselves amongst the most likely candidates for privatization.

The second of Williamson's principles is small numbers bargaining. Clearly, all the monopoly agencies are in the position of having fewer people to compete with for their services. However, the Treasury dependent monopoly agencies such as the Resettlement Agency and the Employment Service are mainly involved in areas where it would be, and is in fact proving to be, relatively easy to generate alternative suppliers. By contrast, the revenue raising monopoly agencies such as Vehicle Inspectorate, the National Weights and Measures Laboratory, Land Registry and the Insolvency Service are all involved in specialist areas where it would be difficult to generate competitive sources of supply. The revenue raising monopoly agencies are therefore more unequivocal monopolies.

The third of Williamson's principles is 'asset specificity', that is where specific skills are required. Specialist skills are clearly more prevalent in the revenue raising agencies in general but it seems that they are marginally more evident in the monopoly revenue raising agencies which includes agencies such as the Hydrographic Office, the National Physical Laboratory and the Intervention Board.

The last two of Williamson's principles are 'bounded rationality', that is, where individuals have limited information or cognitive capacity and 'opportunism', where officials have the tendency to pursue their own interests. These situations are equally likely to arise in all the types of agencies.

Application of Williamson's principles to Next Steps shows that Williamson's hypothesis would be that contract costs are higher for those agencies falling into boxes 1 and 2, that is for those agencies which are most likely to develop furthest as autonomous business units. These agencies are more likely to be involved in specialist functions with specific skills and are less likely to have equivalent organizations who could compete for their work. Application of the Williamson principles identifies these agencies as being in a strong bargaining position in negotiating their framework documents and business plans. Does this mean, however, that the costs of negotiations are likely to be higher, or are other factors such as the interaction of the key personalities responsible for agreeing the 'contracts' more important? These are questions to which we return in Chapter 4.

Conclusions

Despite the fact that Next Steps appears to be a pragmatic initiative rooted more in getting the job done than in history or theory, this chapter has shown that history and theory have played a large part in shaping the development of Next Steps. In many ways then, the development of Next Steps has largely been an incremental process building on past tools, structures and experiences.

Notes

1 Quoted in D.N. McCloskey (1986) *The Rhetoric of Economics*. Brighton, Wheat-sheaf, p. xviii.
2 Para. 303, The Civil Service (1968) *Report of a Management Consultancy Group: Evidence submitted to the Committee under the Chairmanship of Lord Fulton 1966–68*. Vol. 2. London, HMSO.
3 Para. 303, The Civil Service ibid. (1968).
4 Para. 315, The Civil Service ibid. (1968).
5 Para. 316, The Civil Service ibid. (1968).
6 C. Hood (1991) 'Beyond the Public Bureaucracy State? Public Administration in the 1990s', Inaugural lecture, London School of Economics, 16 January.
7 P. Aucoin (1990) Administrative Reform in Public Management: Paradigms, Principles, Paradoxes and Pendulums, *Governance*, 3, 115–37; C. Hood (1990) op. cit.; C. Hood and M. Jackson (1991) *Administrative Argument*. Aldershot, Dartmouth Publishing.
8 National Audit Office (1986) *The Financial Management Initiative*, HC 588. London, HMSO.
9 National Audit Office (1989) *The Next Steps initiative*, HC 410. London, HMSO.
10 Para. 1.4, Cabinet Office (MPO) and HM Treasury (1985) *Non-Departmental Public Bodies: A Guide for Departments*. London, HMSO.
11 Paras 115 and 124, First Report from the Select Committee on Nationalised Industries *Ministerial Control of the Nationalised Industries* (1968) Cmnd. 371 I. London, HMSO.
12 Para. 67, (1980) Report on Non-Departmental Public Bodies, Cmnd. 7797. London, HMSO.
13 Fulton Report op. cit.
14 G. Bamberg and K. Spremann (1989) Prologue in G. Bamberg and K. Spremann, *Agency Theory, Information and Incentives*. Berlin, Springer-Verlag.
15 J. Boston (1992) The Theoretical Underpinnings of Public Sector Restructuring in New Zealand, in J. Boston, J. Martin, J. Pallot and P. Walsh (eds) *Re-shaping the State: New Zealand's Bureaucratic Revolution*. Oxford, Oxford University Press.
16 K. Spremann (1989) Agency Theory and Risk Sharing: Agent and Principal, in G. Bamberg and K. Spremann, op. cit.
17 D. Heymann (1988) 'Input Controls and the Public Sector: What Does Economic Theory Offer?' paper prepared for the Fiscal Affairs Department, International Monetary Fund, Washington DC.
18 W.A. Niskanen (1971) *Bureaucracy and Representative Government*. Chicago, IL, Ardine Atherton; W.A. Niskanen (1973) *Bureaucracy: Servant or Master? Lessons from America*. London, Institute for Economic Affairs; A. Downs (1957) *An Economic Theory of Democracy*. New York, Harper and Row; A. Downs (1967) *Inside Bureaucracy*, Boston, Little, Brown and Company; G. Tullock (1965) *The Politics of Bureaucracy*, Washington DC, Public Affairs Press.
19 For a detailed discussion of the differences between these different strands of public choice theory, see W.C. Mitchell (1988) Virginia, Rochester, and Bloomington: Twenty-five years of Public Choice and Political Science, *Public Choice* 56, 101–119.
20 M. Albrow (1970) *Bureaucracy*. London, Pall Mall.
21 D. Mueller (1979) *Public Choice*. Cambridge, Cambridge University Press.
22 I. McLean (1987) *Public Choice: An Introduction*. Oxford, Basil Blackwell.

23 A. Downs (1960) Why the Government Budget is too Small in a Democracy, *World Politics* 12, 541–64.
24 W.A. Niskanen (1973) op. cit.
25 See work on transaction costs by: R. Coase (1937) The Nature of the Firm, *Economics*, November, 386–407; M.C. Jenson and W.H. Meckling (1976) Theory of the Firm: Managerial Behaviour, Agency Costs and Ownership Structure, *Journal of Financial Economics*, 3, (4), 306–60; D. North (1981) *Structure and Change in Economic History*. New York, Norton; O.E. Williamson (1975) *Markets and Hierarchies*. New York, The Free Press; O.E. Williamson (1985) *The Economic Institutions of Capitalism*. New York, The Free Press.
26 O. Williamson (1975) op. cit.

2

Evolution or revolution?

Slowly, quietly, far from the public spotlight, new kinds of public institutions are emerging. They are lean, decentralized, and innovative. They are flexible, adaptable, quick to learn new ways when conditions change. They use competition, customer choice, and other non-bureaucratic mechanisms to get things done as creatively and effectively as possible. And they are our future.[1]

Although on the face of it, as Chapter 1 has shown, Next Steps is but another in a long line of initiatives aiming to make the executive achieve more for less, there is something more radical about Next Steps which has yet to be explained. Next Steps is more than a repackaging of what has gone before. The Treasury and Civil Service Select Committee heralded Next Steps as 'the most ambitious attempt at civil service reform in the twentieth century'. William Waldegrave, the minister responsible for Next Steps called it 'the quiet revolution'. Next Steps is a powerful initiative that is irrevocably transforming the face of the civil service and its relations with Parliament. This chapter explores what is so special about Next Steps to make it 'revolutionary' when, as we have seen in Chapter 1, it is essentially a repackaging of earlier ideas and characteristics and why this 'revolution' should be an international phenomenon coming at this particular time.

What is so special about Next Steps?

Next Steps is special because it is achieving what earlier reforms have failed to achieve and is transforming the face of Whitehall. It is not just another initiative requiring civil servants to perform certain tasks or collect particular information; it cuts right to the roots questioning the roles of, need for and practices of civil servants in all areas of government – both within agencies and within central departments. Next Steps also has wider implications and is transforming Whitehall's relations with Parliament.

Hardly surprisingly, Next Steps has stirred intense emotions within Whitehall. It has its champions and opponents but few who sit on the fence in apathy. Next Steps has raised expectations and in some cases fear – the expectations of operational managers for delegated powers and the fear of central mandarins of loss of power. Perhaps what gives Next Steps its intensity and strength is not its particular features which, as already noted, are familiar from earlier attempts at reform but rather how these are being applied and their distinctive combination coming together at this particular time.

As we have seen, there is nothing unique about any of the features of Next Steps or the dilemmas which these raise. What is new is the particular combination of these features and the ways in which they are being applied to the civil service.

Separating 'steering from rowing'

There is nothing new about either the idea or the practice of separating 'policy' functions from 'operational' functions, or 'steering from rowing'.[2] The idea is a central core of public choice theory which states that one way of controlling bureaucratic self interest is to separate advisory, regulatory and delivery functions which should be carried out by different agencies. Equally, similar lines of argument have been developed within the management literature. Fifteen years ago Drucker argued for operations to be separated from top management in an arrangement which he termed 'federal decentralization' as it 'makes for strong and effective top managements. It frees top management for the top management tasks'.[3] Drucker saw 'federal decentralization' as an ideal organizational form but one which is only applicable where an organization can truly be divided into a number of 'genuine businesses'.

As the previous chapter has shown, Drucker's ideas of 'federal decentralization' have been applied in government. So, again, there is nothing new about the move to arm's length government and, as the previous chapter has outlined, there is nothing new about the dilemmas it raises of where to draw the line in order to decide on the division of responsibilities, between 'policy' and 'operational' issues and of how to balance the autonomy and accountability of the operational arms to central departments and to Parliament. There is however something new about the ways in which Next Steps is applying the ideas of 'federal decentralization'. The first is its avid application to activities so close to what could, and have, been considered as integral government functions – defence, employment and social security. The second is the use of 'contracts' to structure the new relationships.

Removing core government functions to semi-autonomous units

The earlier moves to create semi-autonomous agencies in the form of the non-departmental public bodies and public corporations involved functions which on the whole were not core government functions but were more freestanding agencies with clearly definable roles, for example, regulatory bodies and agencies which could function in the same way as a business with their results being determined through market performance.

The typology of executive agencies outlined in Chapter 1 shows that some of the Next Steps agencies are also reasonably freestanding agencies, either providing regulatory roles or raising revenues by charging for their goods or services. However, the typology also shows that Next Steps is being applied to parts of the civil service which are politically sensitive, totally dependent on Treasury funding and in some cases also monopoly suppliers. Executive agencies such as the Social Security Benefits Agency can never be a 'business' in the same way as an agency such as Central Office of Information. The Central Office of Information competes with private bodies for the role of providing information services to government departments and it charges for those services to cover its costs. The blueprint for what to do with those agencies which can never really act as a true business with the market controlling their performance is outlined by Drucker:

> We have learned that a great many large companies cannot be divided into genuine businesses . . . simulated decentralization forms units which are not businesses but which are still set up as if they were businesses, with as much autonomy as possible, with their own management and with at least a 'simulation' of profit and loss responsibility. They buy from and sell to each other using 'transfer prices' determined internally rather than by an outside market.[4]

Interestingly, Drucker also outlines some of the shortcomings of 'simulated decentralization' which are that

> a tremendous amount of managerial time and energy will be spent working out the lines between different units that supposedly are autonomous; making sure that they cooperate; mediating between them. The smallest adjustment becomes a top-management decision, a trial of strength, and a matter of honour and sacred principle.[5]

In other words, Drucker's prognosis is that for those agencies closest to the core of government for whom Next Steps is an exercise in 'simulated decentralization' rather than 'federal decentralization', it will be more problematic to distinguish between 'policy' and 'operational' issues and to allow the agencies sufficient autonomy.

The move to contract government

The second feature of Next Steps which is a new departure is the use of contracts to structure the relationships between civil servants. Although the use of contracts and the introduction of the client versus provider divide is now a familiar feature of a number of areas of public policy, the idea has not before been applied to Whitehall.

As Chapter 4 will explore, Next Steps is using contracts to structure the relations: between ministers, central departments and agencies; between agency and agency; and between departments or agencies and the 'outside' supplier. Osborne and Gaebler, the popularizers of the new public management, do not favour contracts within government as 'contracting is one of the most difficult methods a public organisation can choose, because writing and monitoring contracts require so much skill.'[6] They also comment on the high transaction costs that can be involved in any contract arrangement: 'To do it right, cities often spend 20 per cent of the cost of the service on contract management. When they keep services in-house they also have management costs.'[7]

Next Steps is using well tried tools but with two main differences in the ways in which they are being applied. Drucker and Osborne and Gaebler outlined some potential pitfalls in the Next Steps arrangements which, as Chapters 5 and 6 will illustrate, have indeed raised some practical difficulties.

The potency of Next Steps combination of tools

In addition to the innovative ways in which old tools are being applied, a further factor in the Next Steps arrangements which makes the initiative *so* special is its inbuilt defences against any resistance to its changes. The first of these defences is the structural change of creating executive agencies within a contractual framework. This structural change makes the respective roles of central departments and agencies not only more explicit, but also more visible. This means that if, for example, the Treasury were not playing the Next Steps game and delegating agencies with additional 'freedoms', then this failure to play by the Next Steps rules would be blatantly obvious through the published agency framework documents and business plans which outline the boundaries in which agencies must operate. This structural change is an important defence because as we have seen the Financial Management initiative promoted similar notions of delegation within a framework of accountability but these notions were never achieved because of the reluctance of Treasury and other central departments to relinquish any authority.

The second related defence against Next Steps sabotage is the appointment of Next Steps 'champions' in the form of the then Office of the Minister for the Civil Service (which has subsequently been subsumed into the new Office of Public Service and Science) headed by a permanent secretary and now a minister who have the job of ensuring that Next Steps is fully implemented. The first Next Steps champion, the former head of the Next Steps unit, Sir Peter Kemp, was an enigmatic character who was not out of the traditional mandarin mould. The initial success of Next Steps in actually getting off the ground and in seeing the establishment of so many executive agencies was frequently attributed to Kemp's drive for change. Kemp has recently been replaced by a more traditional civil servant from the Ministry of Defence, Richard Mottram, but this replacement took place after Next Steps had been well started and had gained its own momentum.

In summary then, Next Steps is both evolutionary and revolutionary. It is evolutionary because many of its characteristics and tools are not new and are developments of earlier ideas but it is also revolutionary in the ways in which earlier tools are being combined and applied. But why has all this happened now? What has prompted the Next Steps ideas to come to fruition?

Why Next Steps now?

This section considers environmental factors which prompted public service reforms as an international phenomenon and Next Steps in Britain. It then considers why a number of countries have adopted the new public management solutions as their reform strategies.

Political push

The simplistic answer to why Next Steps should have come when it did, with the aims that it did and in the form it did is because of the political push from Lady Thatcher. The Conservative Government and in particular, the now former Prime Minister, Lady Thatcher, has never been a close ally of the civil service. Now that the Conservative Government is embarking on its fourth term in office (under the leadership of John Major), this antipathy is more deeply ingrained and widely sown than was ever previously the case. Surely this is enough to have prompted a major reform of the executive?

Political push is clearly a part of the explanation but does not fully suffice. Next Steps is not unique to Britain. Other western democracies are adopting similar strategies of reform. For example, there are many similarities (and some important differences) in the experiences of Britain, New Zealand and Canada – countries with similar structures. The experiences of New Zealand and Canada and how these compare with Britain will be explored in more detail in Chapter 8. What is important to note here is that Britain, New Zealand and Canada (among other countries) have adopted reform strategies which include a new emphasis on delegation of responsibility and the accompanying shift of emphasis from detailed input controls to output measures. Equally many countries have experienced the new emphasis on performance agreements for unit heads to achieve within a specified level of resources (only in Britain and New Zealand has all this been accompanied by a delegation of accountability to Parliament responsibilities). The emphasis on contracting out and contestability in the provision of public services is also common to other countries. In New Zealand the reforms were introduced under a Labour Government which was elected after the collapse of the previous more right wing government because of the considerable fiscal deficit.

In Britain, Next Steps is also not a 'right wing' phenomenon. There is all party agreement on Next Steps principles and indeed, the ideas which as we have seen were originally enshrined in the Fulton report, were endorsed and promoted in the early 1970s by Labour members such as John Garret MP.

So, although political push has clearly helped in initiating and driving Next Steps and other countries' new public management reforms, it does not fully explain what actually prompted the reforms. It also does not explain why nothing happened 20 years ago when the ideas were being advanced by the likes of John Garret.

The obvious explanation for why the reforms did not happen 20 years ago when the ideas were first discussed is because the necessary tools and structures were not in place 20 years ago to make the ideas easily workable. The evolution of ideas and structures as outlined in the previous chapter combined with technological developments have enabled the refinement of the tools such as the information systems to make the new public management principles more workable.

Development of information technology

Refined information systems are pivotal to the success of the 'new public management'[8] principle of devolution of autonomy but greater accountability for achieving specified ends. In order to decentralize and at the same time ensure greater accountability it is important to have confidence in (centrally) reported performance information.

Taking the example of the Department of Social Security, it certainly did not have the necessary information systems to allow for greater delegation within the existing framework of accountability. However, the comprehensive computerization of social security benefits under the operational strategy coupled with the incremental development of its management and financial management information systems have made the Next Steps principles more implementable within the Department of Social Security.

So, the political push helped the reforms on their way and the tools and structures were vital ingredients to make the reforms workable but this still does not explain what actually catalysed the changes and why there is a degree of international uniformity in the chosen direction of change.

Fiscal crisis

All the countries going down the 'new public management' route are con-cerned about the balance of payments, the size of public expenditure and the cost of state services. A crucial factor in the decision for countries to adopt the 'new public management reforms' therefore appears to be the financial crisis experienced by most developed countries at the time their reform initiatives were launched and established. Common to all the countries is also a crisis of confidence in the image of public services.

In Britain, despite periodic declarations of 'green shoots' , in the summer of 1993 we essentially remain in deep economic recession and have a govern-ment which believes that the way out of this recession is to reduce public expenditure and control inflation. This has inevitably focused attention on the public expenditure programmes, the cost of administering those programmes and on the economy, efficiency and effectiveness of the executive themselves. It has also provided a rationale for marketing public sector cuts and redundancies. We have all heard the rationalization, 'The recession has bitten deep in the private sector and it would be unrealistic for public sector workers that they could ride through without also being affected'. Similarly, the public sector reforms of New Zealand and Canada arose from concern about budget deficits and public sector spending. These concerns are detailed in Chapter 8. A perception of fiscal crisis therefore appears to be a common factor to those countries looking to new public management ideas to reform their public services. There are two explanations for the fact that a number of countries have adopted similar strategies for public sector reform in response to their fiscal crisis.

Improved communications

As communications have developed the world has shrunk and there is an extensive international exchange of ideas between ministers, senior public servants, academics and government advisers. Consequently, there is a greater awareness about what other countries are doing and a keenness to learn from each others' experiences. Academics are travelling the globe talking about the reforms in their own and possibly also in other countries. Public sector officials are also travelling and teams may be sent to look at how well certain ideas are operating in other countries.

Officials are also talking more to each other. An example is the regular 'Five Countries Meeting' where each year, senior civil servants from originally five, and now six countries – Britain, New Zealand, Canada, the USA, Australia, and now Ireland – meet to discuss the progress of their countries' public service reforms, what is working and what is not working and any issues arising. Improved communications therefore, at least in part, explain why different countries are adopting similar strategies of public service reform.

A further factor explaining the degree of convergence in ideas and strategies of reform being adopted by various developed countries is the growth of large international firms of management consultants. They have clearly played an important role in packaging, selling and implementing the 'new public management' reforms. Management consultancy has become big business. The large accountancy based firms have developed into multinational giants which have deeply vested interests in terms of future work, in selling the ideas, language and methods of new public management. The consultancy firms have highly developed international networks through which many of these profitable ideas have been transmitted and translated. The consultancy firms' important role, coupled with the improved direct communications and exchange of ideas between interested parties in various countries, helps to explain not only the uniformity of ideas and principles but also the uniformity of language and practices.

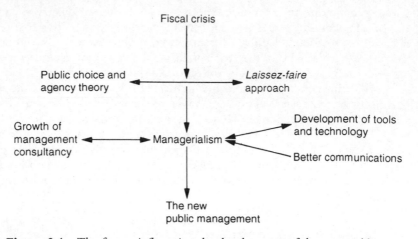

Figure 2.1   The factors influencing the development of the new public management reforms

Conclusions

Tracing the historical development of Next Steps main characteristics elucidates that Next Steps is both evolutionary and revolutionary. It is evolutionary because many of its characteristics are not new and are developments of earlier ideas. It is also revolutionary, however, because of the unique combination of these characteristics and the fact that they have come together at this particular time. Figure 2.1 explores why the ideas have come together at this particular time and why there is a degree of international uniformity in the reform strategies.

Figure 2.1 shows that the relationship between the different factors is by no means straightforward but that there is a pattern of relationships. The fiscal crisis has most likely acted as a catalyst for embracing the *laissez-faire* approach and accordingly, the public choice and agency theories. In this climate managerialism grew (which has prompted the growth of large consulting firms who, in turn, have reinforced the growth in managerialism) and then resulted in the development of the new public management.

Notes

1 D. Osbourne and T. Gaebler (1993) *Reinventing Government: How the Entrepreneurial Spirit is Transforming the Public Sector.* Reading, MA, Addison–Wesley.
2 Ibid., p. 34.
3 P. Drucker (1977) *Management.* London, Pan Books.
4 Ibid., p. 490.

5 Ibid., p. 493.
6 D. Osbourne and T. Gaebler (1993) op. cit., p. 87.
7 Ibid., p. 87.
8 Such reforms have been variously labelled but are most commonly referred to as the 'new public management'. See C. Hood (1990) 'Beyond the Public Bureaucracy State? Public Administration in the 1990s', Inaugural lecture, London School of Economics, 16 January, for an outline of the main features of new public management.

3

Introducing the Department of Social Security and its agencies

In many ways the Department of Social Security is a microcosm of Whitehall as a whole. Examining the evolution of Next Steps within the Department of Social Security therefore enables this book to provide a detailed exploration of the development of Next Steps within a major department whilst also raising issues of wider relevance. As well as being a microcosm, the Department of Social Security presents a major test to the Next Steps principles because it has a high political profile, is a big spender, a large employer and services the whole population at some point in their lives. It is by far the most important department in expenditure terms with a programme expenditure of some £75 billion a year (about a third of all public expenditure) and running costs of nearly £4 billion a year.[1] It has a total staff of around 87,000, a sixth of the entire civil service. Every citizen has at least some contact with the department in their lifetime and the department has the highest public and parliamentary profile – there are more parliamentary questions on social security than on any other subject.

The transformation of the department as a result of Next Steps has been extraordinarily dramatic. Over 98 per cent of the Department of Social Security's staff now work in agencies. The department has so far established five agencies; the Benefits Agency, the Contributions Agency, the Information Technology Services Agency, the Resettlement Agency and the Child Support Agency. In addition, the War Pensions Agency is due to be launched in April 1994. This chapter introduces the Department of Social Security and its agencies and examines the depth of the initial assertion that the Department of Social Security is a microcosm of Whitehall.

Developing Next Steps within the Department of Social Security

What is interesting about the Department of Social Security is that this major administrative change is coming at a time of policy turmoil with the main functions of the department remaining under constant review. What better place to examine the success of the Next Steps principles of dividing responsibility for policy and operational issues and of increasing both autonomy and accountability?

To mention but some of the recent major changes, the department separated from the Department of Health in 1987. 1988 saw the introduction of the new social security regime following 'the most substantial review of the social security since Beveridge'. This review resulted in the introduction of new benefits including income support to replace supplementary benefit and the social fund to replace exceptional needs payments and changes in the eligibility criteria and allowances of existing benefits.

Subsequently, the disablement living allowance has replaced attendance allowance and invalid care allowance for those below pensionable age and there have been other organizational changes such as the establishment of Social Security Centres to take inner city office case work to centres based in areas where there are fewer staffing problems. The department has just handed over responsibility to local authorities for funding people in residential care homes and will also be passing over responsibility for those currently receiving payments from the independent living fund.

The story by no means stops here however; social security spending is currently a main topic for discussion with 'leading experts' meeting for week-end retreats to discuss with ministers issues such as the possibilities of extending the incentives to encourage more people to opt out of the state earnings related pension scheme to take a personal pension and the possibilities of extending employers responsibilities in welfare provision, for example, by making them responsible for the payment of invalidity benefit.

It was against this background of change that the Efficiency Unit report *Improving Management in Government: The Next Steps* was published and its recommendations accepted by the government. Departments were then tasked with identifying likely candidates for executive agency status. The first candidate was relatively easy. The Department of Social Security quickly announced (in February 1988) a small part of its business, the resettlement units, as a candidate for agency status. Identifying other candidates was not quite so easy.

Two internal studies were launched. A report on the department's computer services was carried out by Eric Caines who was then the under-secretary with overall responsibility for these services and on 20 July 1988 the Secretary of State announced an internal study (which became commonly known as the Hickey report – named after the report team leader) conducted with the help of management consultants, with the following terms of reference:

> Taking account of the recommendations in the 'Business of Service' report and the consideration being given to a computer services agency,

to examine the organisation of social security operations and the opportunities for improving service to the public and value to the taxpayer by
creating an executive agency or agencies within the Department of Social
Security, along the lines recommended in the 'Next Steps' report; and to
make recommendations.[2]

Neither of these studies were straightforward or led to unanimously supported
conclusions. With regard to the first of the studies, there were arguments for
and against the computing services being established as a separate agency. The
argument against was that computing services are an integral part of the Department of Social Security. This objection was however overridden by Eric
Caines who was the main drive behind the decision for computing services to
be established as an agency. Eric Caines argued that the computer services
division employed different types of people from other parts of the Department
of Social Security and consequently that existing uniform civil service pay and
conditions were inappropriate.

As regards the second study, the Hickey report, its conclusions were also
not uncontentious. The Hickey report concentrated on the core social security
functions of paying benefits and collecting social security contributions. It first
considered alternatives to agency status such as full scale contracting-out or
privatization but concluded that agency status would offer the right framework
within which to pursue better service and improved efficiency for social
security operations. Ministers' objections to privatization at this stage were
political accountability and sensitivity, confidentiality of personal information,
propriety of public adjudication and lack of suitable outside operators on the
scale required.[3]

The Hickey team tried various models of cutting up social security operations including by client group but they could not find a clear model. The team
therefore argued that social security is a unified business which is 'in a real sense,
one business, not a multiplicity of businesses'[4] which cannot be viewed in
isolation from the political dimension. Indeed, it argued that because the delivery
of social security benefits is in itself subject to close scrutiny by the media and
Parliament, operational managers therefore need to be sensitive to this political
and public dimension. The main thrust of the Hickey report's recommendations
were to recommend a single agency with a chief executive responsible for the
overall management of service delivery and within this to delegate responsibility
to operating units (local offices and individual benefit units). It recommended
that the issue of whether contributions or compliance work should become a
discrete agency should be an issue for future consideration.

Despite the Hickey study's recommendation of a single large agency the
final decision was for the Department of Social Security to establish a separate
Contributions and Benefits Agency. This idea of separating contributions and
benefits was advocated by the permanent secretary, Sir Michael Partridge. A
flavour of his strength of feeling on the issues comes through from his paper on
the experiences of the Department of Social Security,

Table 3.1   The Department of Social Security's agencies

The Benefits Agency

The Benefits Agency is the benefits paying arm of the Department of Social Security and is responsible for paying a wide range of benefits from income support and social fund payments through to child benefit, family credit, pensions, war and widows' pensions, industrial injuries benefits and disability benefits. The Benefits Agency is also responsible for providing relevant information to other bodies to assist in determining entitlement to other benefits such as statutory maternity pay and statutory sick pay, unemployment benefit, housing benefit and legal aid.

The Contributions Agency

The Contributions Agency has two main roles; to ensure that individuals and employers pay the due National Insurance Contributions and to maintain the National Insurance Contribution records, making this information available to the Benefits Agency or the Employment Service when claims are made for contributory benefits such as retirement pensions, unemployment benefits and invalidity benefit. The Inland Revenue collect the bulk of National Insurance Contributions on behalf of the Contributions Agency.

The Information Technology Services Agency

The Information Technology Services Agency provides a wide range of information technology services to the Department of Social Security and to others. Its main aims are to maintain and operate existing systems, to develop new systems and provide consultancy services to the Department of Social Security and its agencies.

The Resettlement Agency

The Resettlement Agency was established to fulfil two apparently conflicting purposes: to manage the facilities for temporary board and lodging provided by the Secretary of State for people without a settled way of life with the aim of influencing them to lead a more settled life and to implement the government's policy of closing Resettlement Units and handing over responsibility for providing alternative facilities to local authorities and voluntary organizations. In effect the agency has the role of running itself down – once it has succeeded in closing down all the resettlement units it ceases to exist.

The Child Support Agency

The Child Support Agency is responsible for implementing the collection of maintenance from all liable relatives in accordance with the new legislation. It provides a legally based service for the assessment, collection and enforcement of maintenance payments in cases where the child's parents are not living together as a family.

The War Pensions Agency

The War Pensions Agency will be established from the Blackpool branch of the Benefits Agency currently responsible for administering war pensions. The agency is to be established from April 1994 but has been running as a unit since the beginning of April 1993. Its main functions are to assess and pay war pensions and allowances, to provide welfare assistance to war pensioners, war widows and their carers and to manage the Ilford Park Polish Home.

Having some experience of contributions policy and operations I know there was no target for collecting contributions and nobody was responsible for setting one. When and where there were staff for the work, they simply applied the law. The policy branch at HQ advised Ministers on policy and prepared legislation. Newcastle Central Office maintained contribution records and sent out deficiency notices to local offices for arrears to be collected. And local office staff did their best to collect what arrears they could . . . This business was ripe for overhaul.[5]

This has brought us to the situation where the Department of Social Security appeared to be diving head first into Next Steps with four executive agencies to be established: the Resettlement Agency, the Information Technology Services Agency, the Benefits Agency and the Contributions Agency, covering over 90 per cent of the department's work.

Two further candidates were to follow; the Child Support Agency stemming from the Child Support Act which was enacted to change the system of maintenance for children and the War Pensions Agency which was first announced as an agency candidate in the Conservative party 1992 election manifesto. Table 3.1 outlines the main functions of the six Department of Social Security's agencies which have been established or announced so far.

Clearly the agencies have different although interrelated aims but more importantly they differ in other respects. It is precisely these differences which enable us to test the Next Steps principles in a variety of settings. The Department of Social Security is a useful laboratory to investigate the influence of various factors on the development of agencies more generally. The Department of Social Security's agencies differ in their stages of development, in size, in amount of expenditure and administrative costs, in whether or not their 'business' generates revenue, in their financial regimes and in the personalities involved – some are headed by chief executives who have come from outside the civil service. Table 3.2 summarizes the main features of the Department of Social Security's agencies. It outlines the main differences between the agencies which enable us to draw wider conclusions about the development of Next Steps in general. The table also includes information on the departmental headquarters which we will come to discuss later in the chapter.

Stage of development

An agency's stage of development is an important factor in any examination of the progress of Next Steps. Agencies cannot be set up overnight. The first step is the structural change of actually creating the agency and establishing the management and organizational structures. The second step is the development and refinement of the internal supporting structures including the management and financial management information systems. Clearly the issues facing an agency in its early stages of development are different from those facing a mature agency. The Department of Social Security's agencies provide a useful

Table 3.2 The Department of Social Security and its agencies

	Launch Date	Staff Numbers	Annual Operative Costs £M	Annual Programme Expenditure £M	Financial Regime	Chief Executive Grade	Chief Executive Origin
Benefits Agency	April 1991	69,377	1,453	74,140	gross running cost control	2	chief executive Gloucestershire County Council
Contributions Agency	April 1991	9,505	137	not applicable	gross running cost control	4	civil servant (in post)
Resettlement Agency	May 1989	533	28	not applicable	gross running cost control	6	civil servant (in post)
Information Technology Services Agency	April 1990	4,442	384	not applicable	gross running cost control[3]	3	a) civil servant (Ministry of Defence) b) civil servant[4] (Benefits Agency)
Child Support Agency	April 1993	2,398	121	not applicable	gross running cost control	4	health service management, then, Director of MIND
War Pensions Agency	April 1994	not yet known	27[1]	not yet known	gross running cost control	not yet known	not yet known
Headquarters	not applicable	1,421	603[2]	not applicable	not applicable	1	not applicable

1992/93 figures from *Social Security Departmental Report: The Government's Expenditure Plans 1993–94 to 1995–96*, Cm 2213. London, HMSO.

Notes: 1 War Pensions Unit running costs 1992–93. 2 includes £521 M administered centrally by the department and not by a particular agency. 3 plans to move to net cost controls. 4 chief executive was replaced in 1993.

cross section of agencies in various stages of development. First, as Table 3.2 shows, the Department of Social Security's agencies were established over a period of five years from May 1989 to April 1994. Second, even on becoming an agency they are all at very different stages of development. In this respect the case study of the Department of Social Security and its agencies will therefore not be atypical overall even if it is so at the extreme ends of its spectrum of agencies.

At the one end of the spectrum lies the Child Support Agency which is an extreme example of an agency with a lot of work to do. In effect the agency is starting almost from scratch and, unlike most other agencies is not inheriting existing organizational structures, people and ways of doing things. It inherited an Act of Parliament. The Department of Social Security and subsequently the Benefits Agency did hold responsibility for collecting maintenance from the liable relatives of those claiming benefit but this will only be one aspect of the new agency's work.

At the other extreme of the spectrum lies the Benefits Agency which, on face, would appear relatively advanced as it inherited existing organizational structures and much of the existing departmental management and financial management information which related particularly to areas of work which became the responsibility of the Benefits Agency. However, despite appearances, the Benefits Agency has also had considerable work in reorganizing itself to best suit its 'business needs' and in establishing the necessary structures and information systems. For example, when the Benefits Agency was created, the seven remaining regional offices were abolished and the central office and local office structures were integrated under a unified command. As the agency developed, structural change continued. Only recently were there some changes to the structure and role of the Benefits Agency management board. The changes were made to create a smaller board with the aim of bridging the divide between the agency's headquarters and field operations. Also, as Chapter 4 will demonstrate, despite appearances, the Benefits Agency had considerable work to do in developing its management and financial management information.

In between, we have the Contributions Agency. Contributions work used to be dispersed throughout the country with staff based in social security local offices. Contributions staff used to form a part of the organizational hierarchy of the offices in which they were based. One of the first tasks in planning the Contributions Agency was therefore to establish an organizational hierarchy. This was aided by the centralization of those contributions staff who used to be based throughout the local office network. Most of the staff now work in the central Newcastle upon Tyne site.

The department's computing division also used to be dispersed throughout the country and did not have its own organizational hierarchy. However, even prior to Next Steps, the Information Technology Services Directorate was formed which was a distinct computing unit within the department. The Information Technology Services Directorate was also already competing for some of its work with outside contractors. However, as Chapter 4 will show, considerable work was necessary to develop appropriate information systems to meet with Next Steps requirements. Indeed, the Information Technology Services Division was nearly not launched as an agency because of the Treasury's concerns about the quality of the available financial information and the fact that there was no means of measuring improvements in efficiency.

The Resettlement Agency was also a relatively developed agency in the sense that the agency functions were already operating as a distinct division within the department. However, there was considerable work to be done mainly because of a lack of adequate management information. As the department's Permanent Secretary put it,

> Defining its [the Resettlement Agency's] objectives and writing its framework document of responsibilities and its first annual business plan proved a major task, since it brought out starkly the inconsistencies in policies and practices with which it had been operating for many years. If the main objective was to resettle its 'customers' back into society, where were the targets or the information on how many had been successfully resettled? What counted as 'successful' resettlement? Not returning to one of our resettlement centres within a specified period? For how long?[6]

Size

Figure 3.1 shows that the Department of Social Security's agencies vary considerably by size. The Benefits Agency is by far the largest of all the executive agencies and employs some 70,000 staff. Its annual programme expenditures stand at some £74 billion and it has annual operative costs of nearly £1.5 billion. The Contributions Agency is also a relatively large agency employing some 9,500 staff and having annual operative costs of £137 million. By contrast the Resettlement Agency employs just over 500 staff and has annual operative costs of less than £30 million. These contrasts in the sizes of the Department of Social Security's agencies enable us to explore whether size makes any difference.

Financial regime and whether the 'business' generates revenue

Figure 3.1 also illustrates how the Department of Social Security's agencies range across the spectrum of agencies types and again therefore as a case study, raise issues of wider relevance.

Box A, Treasury dependent monopoly agencies

There are two distinct categories of agencies in box A, both of which are clearly core government functions, those that spend exchequer money and

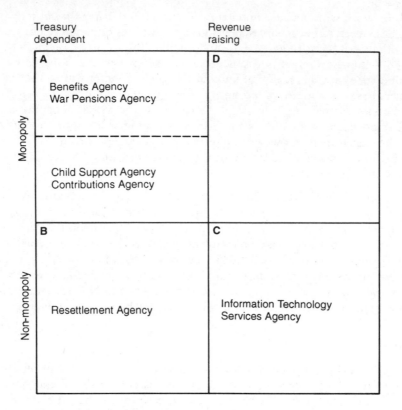

Figure 3.1 Typology of Department of Social Security agencies

those that collect exchequer revenues. The Benefits Agency and the future War Pensions Agency fall into the first of these categories. There are limitations in the extent to which these agencies can become 'businesses' as they provide fundamental public services and are entirely dependent on exchequer funding. The nature of the agencies in these categories does not however mean that they cannot adopt some of the private sector language and methods promoted by Next Steps, but it does mean that they are limited in the extent to which they can go down the road of concentrating on bottom line balance sheets. For example, although the main business of the Benefits Agency is paying out social security benefits, the agency is thinking about ways it can generate revenue from other subsidiary functions. For example, it is thinking about how it can generate income from the medical examinations which it carries out for people going abroad and from selling its training courses for staff in local offices, such as one on how to deal with violent people, to local authorities. The fact that these agencies are almost entirely dependent on exchequer funding is also likely to affect their degree of autonomy from Treasury and departmental headquarters' financial and management controls as the Treasury will be reluctant to allow additional freedoms which may result in increases in public expenditure. As an important aside, these agencies are also those which attract a high degree of media, public and political interest which again is likely to restrict their ability to develop as semi-autonomous units.

Some of the same issues apply to the other agencies in box A, the revenue raisers. In the case of the Department of Social Security we have two agencies in this category, the Contributions Agency and the Child Support Agency. Again the revenue raisers are core government functions but there would possibly be less difficulty with contracting out large parts of their functions such as the collection of national insurance contributions from the self-employed.

Box B, Vote funded non-monopoly agencies

Across the board of all the Next Steps agencies there are few agencies in the box B category in general and returning to our case study of the Department of Social Security, there is only one agency in this category – the Resettlement Agency. The agencies in this category are non-essential (as there are others in their line of business) but mostly government funded activities. This dispensibility explains why the present drive to reduce the size of government falls heavily on agencies in this category. Turned around, we are saying that agencies in this category are unlikely to continue as arms of government. Accordingly, the Resettlement Agency has the aim,

> to disengage the Government from the direct management of the hostels either by replacing them with more appropriate facilities or by making capital and revenue grants available to voluntary organisations and local authorities who may wish to purchase them and provide similar resettlement services.[7]

In other words, one of the main aims of the Resettlement Agency is to close itself down and hand over responsibilities for its functions (and possibly its buildings) to local authorities or to voluntary organizations.

Box C, Revenue raising non-monopoly agencies

In some ways the agencies in this category are potentially the most interesting so far as the development of Next Steps is concerned, particularly when it is also considered in the light of the current 'Competing for Markets' initiative which may result in the contracting-out of large parts of existing government functions. These are the agencies which generate revenue from their services, possibly to the extent of covering all of their costs, and who have other bodies working in the same field who may be contracted to carry out large parts or possibly all of the agencies' existing functions.

As far as our case study of the Department of Social Security is concerned, in this category we have the Information Technology Services Agency. The main issue facing the Information Technology Services Agency is that it has had to develop the information systems to find out the unit costs of its services so it can charge to cover the costs of its services. There are plans for it to move to a net cost accounting system which will mean that it will have more financial freedoms. However, more importantly, it is increasingly having to compete for much of its work with other contractors. Indeed, there are plans for the Information Technology Services Agency to reduce to about 10 per cent of its original size with the core being retained to advise on the policy implications of developing information technology within the department and to manage contracts.

Box D, Revenue raising monopolies

In general the issues facing the agencies in this category may be very similar to those being addressed by the agencies in category C with the exception that it may be difficult, at least initially, to find contractors to take on large parts of the work of the agencies in this category.

Personalities

A further factor which may affect the development of an agency are the personalities and outlooks of the people in the key posts. One indicator of this is the backgrounds of the chief executives and possibly of other key agency staff. As Table 3.2 illustrates, again in this respect the case study of the Department of Social Security provides a cross section. The Department of Social Security's agencies are headed by chief executives from a variety of backgrounds, some within the civil service and some from outside.

The role of headquarters

The introduction to our case study of the Department of Social Security would not be complete without an introduction to the department's headquarters. One of the main tasks facing the Department of Social Security has been to define the role and structure of headquarters. Questions over the appropriate role of headquarters have continued both within headquarters and within the department's agencies from the early days of Next Steps' development within the department. Often these questions have run deep. What holds the Department of Social Security together? Are its 'shared values' really shared values or a series of statements about its business and aims?

   These philosophical exercises at management board 'awaydays' have led to some important questions about the role of headquarters. Should the role of headquarters be like a distinct agency with its own discrete functions to perform? Indeed, should it have its own framework document and business plan? Should the role be to oversee the agencies? To coordinate developments within the department to ensure parity and the continuance of social security as a 'single department'? To act as arbiter in any disputes between

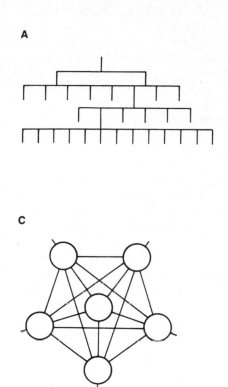

A

B

C

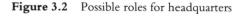

Figure 3.2   Possible roles for headquarters

agencies (possibly with the aim of protecting the interests of the smaller agencies against those of their larger opponents with higher grades of staff)? These roles are of course not all entirely conflicting. Most of these questions have not been overtly answered within the department, although it is apparent that senior headquarters people are clearly of the opinion that the department must remain as a 'single department'. These arguments are defended with assertions about agency interdependence and political sensitivity but are possibly also influenced by factors such as the fact that senior headquarters staff are largely home grown, having mainly developed their careers within the department.

The effect of this strong notion of a 'single department' is that the Department of Social Security has so far moved from the classic Weberian hierarchy (model A in Figure 3.2) to model B rather than to model C, where the agencies would have a greater degree of autonomy both in their dealings with each other and with outside parties.

Headquarters has now been reorganized in recognition of the fact that it performs three main functions: policy work in support of ministers; corporate management of the department as a whole and legal services. As an aside, the legal section operates rather like a separate agency. The departmental management board has also been reorganized. The board now consists of the Permanent Secretary, his deputy secretaries, all the department's agency chief executives and the non-executive directors. The aim is that the agency chief executives sit on the board as managers of the department as a whole and not primarily in their capacity as heads of agencies. They discuss 'strategic issues' about the future development of the department.

Conclusions

Returning to our original assertion, do the Department of Social Security's agencies form a microcosm of the development of executive agencies across the board or is there something different about the Department of Social Security which may result in its experiences being atypical? Is there a Department of Social Security factor?

This chapter has shown that the answer to both these questions is a resounding 'yes'. The Department of Social Security's agencies range across the spectrum of agency 'types' and therefore raise issues of wider relevance. There are many points raised by the case study which can be applied more generally. However, there is also a Department of Social Security factor. The case study also identifies distinctive features such as the concern with a 'single department'.

Notes

1 Figures 1992–93 estimated outturn 'from: *Social Security Departmental Report: The Government's Expenditure Plans 1993–94 to 95–96* (1993) Cm 2213. London, HMSO.
2 Para. 1.4, Department of Social Security (1989) *Agency Study Report*. Unpublished report.
3 Sir M. Partridge *Next Steps and Executive Agencies, Privatisation and Contracting Out*, (forthcoming) in D. Falconer (ed.) *Public Administration and Public Employment in the 1990s*. London, Oxford University Press.
4 Para. 2.8, Department of Social Security (1989) op. cit.
5 Para. 26, Sir M. Partridge (forthcoming) op. cit.
6 Para. 21, Sir M. Partridge (forthcoming) op. cit.
7 Para. 240, *Social Security Departmental Report* (1993) op. cit.

4

The main organizational actors in the Next Steps power struggle

As we have seen Next Steps is about transforming the boundaries of responsibilities across Whitehall. The Efficiency Unit report which launched Next Steps set out the bare bones of the changes but provided little detail about who should be doing what. Such important unanswered questions effectively left Next Steps open to manipulation.

This chapter examines the changing roles and relationships between the various organizational actors shaping the development of Next Steps. It introduces the different players, outlines their stakes in the Next Steps arena and explores the influence of each of these players in shaping the development of Next Steps. It does this by first introducing the various players and then by examining their respective roles in some case studies of Next Steps development.

Introducing the players in the Next Steps arena

There are two main sets of actors in the Next Steps arena – the Whitehall actors and the parliamentary actors. The Whitehall actors are those who are either responsible for implementing the initiative or whose powers, responsibilities and working environments are directly affected by the initiative. The parliamentary actors are those who use the executive to carry out their policies and those who are responsible for securing the executive's accountability to Parliament. This section sets out who these actors are and briefly sets out their stance in the Next Steps arena.

When Next Steps was adopted as government policy it was placed under the wing of the then Office of the Minister for the Civil Service (OMCS) which has subsequently been assimilated into the Office of Public Service and Science (OPSS). Effectively the OMCS was appointed as Next Steps champion. Its role has been to chivvy departments into identifying possible candidates for agency status, to aid the establishment of these agencies and to ensure that agencies have the appropriate freedoms to allow Next Steps to develop.

The Treasury's first priority continues to be the control of public expenditure. This overriding concern creates a tension between the OPSS and the Treasury. The OPSS is keen to launch agencies and give them freedoms whilst the Treasury want to be sure about agencies' 'track records' and reporting arrangements before it is willing to take a 'hands-off approach'.

Parent departments also have an interest in resisting the development of Next Steps on the grounds that it could erode their empires and powers. The basic premiss of Next Steps is to devolve power from the centre and to leave agency managers free to run the day to day operations of their agencies. Particularly as Next Steps develops to the stage where most operational functions are devolved to agencies this raises questions over the appropriate roles and powers of those remaining in headquarters.

By contrast, the expectation would be that chief executives and agency staff would regard Next Steps as a major coup. Next Steps is about taking power from the centre and devolving it to the new agencies. The term 'chief executive' suggests that the new heads of the agencies are responsible for running their own empires relatively free from the traditional Whitehall constraints of upwards reporting.

The other main Whitehall actors involved in the development of Next Steps are the trade unions. There has been a fundamental difference in the approaches taken by the three main civil service unions to Next Steps – the First Division Association (FDA), the Civil and Public Servants Association (CPSA) and the National Union of Civil and Public Servants (NUCPS). The FDA and the CPSA declared their neutrality on the Next Steps programme whereas NUCPS opposed the changes. The unions have put in a bid to influence the development of Next Steps but this stake has been marginalized by careful management on the part of other Whitehall players and the fact that the trade unions' stronghold on the civil service has steadily reduced over the last 10 years.

The parliamentary actors in the Next Steps arena include ministers, Members of Parliament, the Public Accounts Committee supported by the National Audit Office and the Select Committees. Ministers can play an important, if sometimes subtle, role in shaping the development of Next Steps as their personalities, interests and political stance can act to influence the initiative's progress in their departments. Members of Parliament can exert their power on the development of Next Steps either through House of Commons debates or through the use of oral or written parliamentary questions. The Public Accounts Committee and the Select Committees can exert their power through examining the progress of the initiative.

Shaping the development of Next Steps

The Office of the Minister for the Civil Service (OMCS)/ Office of Public Service and Science (OPSS)

The OMCS was staffed by bright young civil servants on secondment from their departments and headed by Sir Peter Kemp. The early role of OMCS was to actively encourage departments to identify possible candidates for agency status and to aid the establishment of these agencies. Kemp had a high profile and was by no means a traditional Whitehall civil servant. As Colin Hughes of the *Independent* put it,

> Anyone who needs a fast acting antidote to the received *Yes Minister* image of senior career civil servants need only spend an hour with Peter Kemp. His quickfire speech is as brisk as a racing commentator's. Rarely, if ever, does he duck or sidestep a question. And – perhaps the biggest shock of all – if he does not know the answers, he says so.[1]

Kemp became commonly regarded (at least in Whitehall circles) as a main reason for Next Steps effectively taking root. His job was to get Next Steps off the ground and to overcome any Whitehall resistance. The Next Steps team was actively involved in encouraging departments to identify agency candidates and in establishing the executive functions as agencies (after first considering prior options, that is, whether privatization or contractorization would be a more appropriate course of action). OMCS issued guidance to departments on issues such as identifying candidates for agency status and on thinking about what should be in their framework agreements.

OMCS also played a role in reviewing options to maintain the momentum of Next Steps. The Efficiency Unit report of 1991, commonly known as the Fraser report, focused on relations between departments and their agencies.[2] The report documents how OMCS's aims were tempered by other powerful Whitehall interests, notably by parent departments and by the Treasury. One of the main recommendations of the Fraser report was,

> The objective should be to move to a position where agency Framework Documents establish that, within the overall disciplines of the cash limits and targets set managers are free to make their own decisions on the management of staff and resources except for any specifically reserved areas. The exclusion of any area from the Chief Executive's authority should be positively justified. In order to achieve further progress in delegation, a first objective should be to revise Framework Documents on these lines at the first three year review of each agency. This does not rule out an earlier review if the Chief Executive or sponsor Department considers it timely. The Order in Council should be amended at the earliest opportunity to permit such delegation.[3]

In other words, the Fraser report aimed to provide agencies with maximum delegation through only specifying in their framework documents what the agencies cannot do rather than what they can do. The recommendation was a recognition of the unsatisfactory nature of the existing status quo for the future development of Next Steps. Agencies were not being allowed the necessary freedoms.

The Order in Council was not amended to allow for the development of these 'upside down' Framework Documents. Following the Efficiency Unit's recommendation, a team from the Civil Service College was commissioned to investigate the feasibility of introducing upside down framework documents. The team identified some practical difficulties with the notion of the Framework Documents specifying everything that an agency could not do. The team also found considerable resistance to the idea from parent departments and from the Treasury. The Efficiency Unit report was not popular amongst some headquarters people. One senior headquarters official informed me that the Efficiency Unit report was 'the worst thing ever to have come out of the Efficiency Unit'.[4]

By contrast, the report was generally popular amongst agency officials. Feelings seemed to be summed up by a senior agency official who described the Fraser report as 'a missed opportunity'.[5]

After the 1992 general election, Next Steps, along with the Citizen's Charter, the Market Testing initiative and the Efficiency Unit were moved together to create the Office of Public Service and Science under the ministerial direction of William Waldegrave. The rationale was to bring together the reform initiatives under one roof. The new department is much bigger than the old OMCS which is reflected in the budget which changed from some £100 million a year to some £1.2 billion. Shortly after this reorganization, there was a shuffling of senior civil servants with the outcome that the Permanent Secretary, Sir Peter Kemp was replaced by a traditional civil servant, Richard Mottram from the Ministry of Defence. Two reasons have come out of Whitehall for the demise of Kemp. The first is that there was a personality clash between the new minister, William Waldegrave and Kemp. The second explanation is that Kemp had the right skills for launching Next Steps and had achieved this goal but did not have the right skills for the next stage of the initiative or for running a large department.

The change of leadership could have potentially changed the balance of power between the Whitehall actors in shaping the development of Next Steps. Next Steps no longer has Kemp or an equivalent as a champion to defend it from 'traditionalists'. Mottram is not so directly involved in Next Steps as his predecessor. The Next Steps team say that they had at least daily contact with Kemp whereas they do not normally have daily contact with Mottram. The Next Steps team do not however see the loss of Kemp as a particular problem because they see that the initiative now has its own impetus.

The Treasury

OMCS made friends as well as enemies in Whitehall. At least in the early days of Next Steps the main source of resistance was OMCS's neighbour, the

Treasury. As holder of the purse strings and employer of the cream of White-hall, the Treasury has always been the great power of Whitehall. The Treasury was initially rather reticent about Next Steps. It was concerned that allowing agencies autonomy and flexibility could have adverse effects on its financial control and ultimately its power base. It did not take too long however, for this reticence to change to cautious support. The change occurred when the Treasury began to realize that, handled correctly, Next Steps should bring about better value for money which is in everybody's interests but more importantly, that it could also help establish better control arrangements. As one Treasury official pointed out, 'Ironically the process of launching something as an agency often results in us being more involved in the detail of that operation.'[6]

Role of the Treasury in developing monitoring arrangements

Before an executive function can be launched as an agency, the Treasury must be satisfied that the financial and management information systems and report-ing arrangements are adequate. This provides them with the opportunity to review the adequacy of the information they require. The Treasury expects to be involved from the early stages of agency development: in drafting Frame-work Documents and planning and developing of performance measures and key targets. The Treasury's officials suggested two possible explanations as to why the Treasury has become so involved in the detail of developing agency performance measures. The first is that departmental headquarters may have difficulty initially in fulfilling this role, partly because significant in-house expertise on performance measurement is being passed to agencies and conse-quently there may be insufficient expertise remaining within many departmen-tal headquarters for monitoring performance. The second is that department headquarters 'may be adopting an overly hands-off approach to this role, at least regarding agency technical questions'.[7] Whatever the explanation for their intense involvement, it means that Treasury officials play a central role in shaping the development of Next Steps.

The Treasury has the role of ensuring that all the necessary structures are in place before an agency can be launched. This role includes advising on whether the accounting systems can be brought up to scratch. The Department of Social Security's Information Technology Services Agency was nearly not launched as an agency in April 1990, as planned, because of the Treasury's concerns about the department's and its own capabilities for monitoring 'the success of the agency. The Treasury expressed two main concerns: first, there was no means of measuring efficiency improvements and second, existing systems were limited in the extent to which they could measure achievement. These concerns were magnified by the fact that the Information Technology Services Agency had clear ideas on how it saw its development and the Trea-sury and the Department of Social Security's headquarters were concerned about having the means to monitor adequately the new agency's performance.

The management consultancy firm, Price Waterhouse, had been commissioned by the Department of Social Security to report on appropriate performance measures and targets for the Contributions Agency and the Information Technology Services Agency. Price Waterhouse believes that its work provided the necessary assurances to the Treasury to enable the development of adequate performance measures and monitoring arrangements and to allow the Information Technology Services Unit to become an agency.

Equally, once agencies are up and running, departments and agencies must agree with the Treasury what monitoring information on their agencies' performance measures and targets will be made available to the Treasury. For all except the most significant agencies, the Treasury does not formally approve these measures and targets but informally plays an important role in influencing the information produced and reported.

Role of the Treasury in approving agencies' financial and personnel flexibilities

The Treasury also has the role of adjudicating the scope and form of the financial and personnel flexibilities to be delegated to agencies. Normal practice is for agencies and departments first to agree and outline the extent of desired flexibilities and for the Treasury to evaluate the proposals and to make the ruling. Examples of the areas for which agencies have been negotiating additional flexibilities include the financial flexibilities to carry over money, to move money between budgets and to make capital purchases without prior consultation; to directly recruit up to certain grades and to establish their own pay and grading arrangements. Concentrating on the delegation of pay and grading decisions illustrates the pivotal role of the Treasury in the negotiations.

The arrangements for negotiating pay and grading flexibilities have evolved since 1988. Originally departments and agencies had the job of formulating proposals and presenting these to the Treasury. The Treasury is now taking a more active role in encouraging agencies and departments to devise proposals for such arrangements. The Treasury deals directly with agencies and with agencies' departmental headquarters and decides, on the basis of the agency's investment appraisal, whether proposals for new pay and grading arrangements will bring about overall savings (resulting from greater efficiency). The Treasury makes the decisions in these negotiations and confesses to being more cautious where agencies are totally dependent on the Treasury for funding and face few competitive pressures.

These examples illustrate that Next Steps has not, as the Treasury initially feared, weakened central financial controls or undermined its powers. The Treasury has carved itself out a central role in ensuring that the planning and management systems are in place before agencies are granted additional flexibilities. The examples illustrate that the Treasury has slowly been allowing agencies greater flexibility as Next Steps has developed and it seems likely that the next stage of development will see a significant increase in agency autonomy and flexibility. If the Treasury does grant significant additional 'flexibilities' it will in part be due to pressure from OPSS but it seems likely that it will also reflect the Treasury's recognition of agencies' ability to cope with the additional flexibilities and confidence in the reporting arrangements.

Departmental headquarters

There has clearly been some resistance to Next Steps by departmental headquarters. In the case of the Department of Social Security, some of this resistance has been packaged up as the need for the Department of Social Security to remain as a *single department* and for departmental headquarters to continue to play an active interventionist role in order to protect staff mobility and the smaller agencies. This approach is outlined in the Department of Social Security's 1993 annual report:

> While seeking to take maximum advantage of the freedoms offered by central initiatives such as Next Steps, the Department remains a single organisation with interlinked businesses and a shared set of management purposes and aims which underpin the wider aims and objectives of the social security programme . . .
>
> Belonging to a wide group brings advantages. The Departmental Board, chaired by the Permanent Secretary sets the strategic direction for the Department as a whole and develops common policies, e.g., on purchasing and market testing. It is taking a coordinated approach to the development of a departmental information systems strategy. The business units of the Department have also agreed a common approach in a number of personnel areas. These guiding principles provide a framework within which business units can develop their own personnel practices taking account of the wider interest of the Department and the career development needs of its staff'.[8]

It is difficult to disentangle the motivations behind these arguments but loss of personal power by senior headquarters people is clearly shaping the arguments and consequently the future development of Next Steps. It is not however possible to talk of 'headquarters' as a single entity. Different views and different approaches have emerged from the various parts of headquarters. Again drawing on the experience of the Department of Social Security it seems the finance division have been the most concerned about allowing too much flexibility without first ensuring that 'sufficient' checks are in place.

The resistance to Next Steps is not however as strong amongst senior headquarters civil servants as could be expected. Sir Peter Kemp provided two explanations for this. First, he argued that there is a new breed of people in the top echelons of the civil service. This new breed joined in the 1960s and grew up to think differently from their predecessors. They are more aware of costs and more open to change. He said that by contrast, those who were in senior posts at the time of Fulton had joined the civil service in the 1930s/40s and had developed their careers in the honeymoon time following the Second World War where economic constraints did not dominate the agenda. Second, he argued that the changes throughout the 1980s paved the way for Next Steps by developing an appropriate management culture.[9] Possibly departmental headquarters see Next Steps as an inevitable and not unexpected development which is to be treated not with scorn but rather as an exercise in damage limitation.

The executive agencies

Certainly the Department of Social Security's agencies have been generally very favourable to Next Steps and this has caused some tensions with departmental headquarters. Indeed, a senior department of social security official explained the permanent secretary's, Sir Michael Partridge's, fixation with the idea of a single department as a reaction to 'some potentially embarrassing go-it-alone gung-hoery by the Benefits Agency recently'.[10]

The chief executive of the Benefits Agency, Michael Bichard, has had to sign up to this idea of a single department but it is clear that he sees it as a real threat, because it could stifle the kind of corporate identity and initiative that he regards himself as there to foster. Indeed, one of the other Department of Social Security agency chief executives asserted that the term single department is 'code for watching people'.[11]

Perhaps not surprisingly there have been some tensions between the Department of Social Security's agencies and headquarters. Some of these have been teething problems in establishing the new structures and defining respective responsibilities. An example of this relates to the review of the Contributions Agency's high level targets. The Department of Social Security's headquarters and the Contributions Agency were agreed that there was a need for a review because earlier targets had in some cases become inappropriate and because existing targets did not reflect some important aspects of the work of the agency. The Contributions Agency began the work of reviewing the targets and devising new ones with the intention of agreeing this with headquarters' Corporate Management Division. Meanwhile, headquarters' Corporate Management Division carried out a review of the targets and placed an item on the Contributions Agency management board agenda to agree to these targets. The headquarters' intention was that the Contributions Agency would sign up to those targets at that meeting. The Contributions Agency was not happy with this. It did not agree with the targets themselves but more importantly it was displeased that responsibility for reviewing the targets had switched from the Contributions Agency to headquarters and that headquarters had put an item on the Agency Management Board's agenda. The Contributions Agency actually won this battle on a point of procedure – the fact that the department should not have tabled the item on the Agency Management Board agenda.

There are however clear differences between the agencies in their starting points and expectations for development and consequently the nature of their relations with the Department of Social Security's headquarters. This point is illustrated by a comment from the chief executive of the new Child Support Agency who said that in drawing up the agency framework document, 'I want to get my toe in the door in the area of flexibilities but I don't want to seek too much at this stage as there is much else to do.'[12] The chief executive pointed out why she feels differently from the other Department of Social Security agency chief executives on the issue of flexibilities:

> Most agencies have inherited staff and structures and therefore seek flexibilities to bring about change. I have inherited an Act of Parliament and a small project team. The Child Support Agency still has some enormous constraints but it does not regard them in the same way. One needs to be pragmatic within the system.[13]

In addition to the tensions between headquarters and agencies there have also been some tensions between agencies. Feelings have been running so high between the agencies that some apparently fairly trivial issues have risen to high levels for resolution. A good example of this is how the telephones should be answered at the large Newcastle Social Security site which now houses staff from the Benefits Agency, the Contributions Agency and the Information Technology Services Agency. The switchboard (which is a part of the Benefits Agency but which also provides the service for the other agencies on site) used to answer the telephone, 'Department of Social Security'. After Next Steps was launched, to the annoyance of the other agencies, the switchboard answered the telephone, 'Benefits Agency'. There was much discussion between the agencies on the issue and eventually it went up to the level of Permanent Secretary for arbitration. Those phoning the Newcastle agencies will now be greeted with, 'Benefits Agency, Contributions Agency and Information Technology Services Agency'! Other teething problems between agencies have related to issues of accommodation, car parking and also to territorial issues of responsibilities for functions.

There has been some movement of functions between the Department of Social Security's agencies but one incident where there was disagreement between the agencies related to the responsibility for payment of overseas pensions. These were dealt with by the Contributions Agency but the Benefits Agency then made a pitch for the work. Again, headquarters acted as arbiter and ruled that the work should remain with the Contributions Agency. Many of the tensions between agencies and others cited here are clearly teething problems but there is a longer term issue about the appropriate role of the department both in its relations to its agencies and in its involvement in relations between agencies.

Trade unions

In so far as Next Steps is a power struggle between the organizational actors it seems that the trade unions have lost. The efforts of the National Union for

Civil and Public Servants (NUCPS), the civil service union which explicitly opposed Next Steps, and of the Civil and Public Servants Association (CPSA) had little effect in arresting or influencing its development and overall, Next Steps resulted in a loss of union power.

Certainly in the case of the Department of Social Security, there was little disruption in the way of industrial action or 'work to rules' and the emerging shape of Next Steps hardly appears to reflect the trade unions' interests. Agencies have been established, reviews are well underway to develop separate agency pay and grading structures, more people are being appointed from outside on short term appointments and the market testing programme is well underway with the Department of Social Security agencies due to report on the decisions on whether they plan to contract out their support services by the end of 1993. Closer to home, the amount of facility time available to trade union representatives has been drastically reduced. In 1990 the Department of Social Security had over 90 trade union representatives with 100 per cent facility time, that is, they worked entirely on trade union business. Now, all trade union representatives are required to work at least 50 per cent of their time on official duties and they must report how they have used their facility time.

With the exception of market testing, there has been relatively little opposition to these changes from the trade unions. For example, the days lost to industrial action in the Benefits Agency were drastically reduced from around 30,000 a year to 1,600 in 1992/93. The Benefits Agency personnel director explained that the fall,

> can be explained at least in part by the state of the economy and the declining influence of unions generally. But it was also a result of the Benefits Agency restructuring. By removing the regional tier, management and unions now discuss matters at the point where people are empowered to make decisions. All this has been possible because, up until recent events, the majority of staff have not been greatly concerned with the changes.[14]

In summary then, it appears that the trade unions have so far not been a major player in the Next Steps power struggle mainly because staff's main concerns have been whether or not they will continue to have a job tomorrow rather than the ins and outs of the Next Steps agreements. However, as demonstrated recently (in July 1993), when around 30,000 staff took industrial action, the market testing programme has created renewed enthusiasm amongst staff for trade unions because of the possibility that it could put staff jobs in jeopardy.

The parliamentary actors

The parliamentary actors in the Next Steps arena include ministers, Members of Parliament, the Public Accounts Committee supported by the National Audit Office (NAO) and the Select Committees. This section outlines the varying roles played by these people in shaping the development of the Next Steps initiative.

Departmental ministers clearly play an important and sometimes subtle role in shaping the development of Next Steps. Their personalities, interests and political stance can act to influence the initiative's progress in their departments. For example, ministers can influence which chief executives are appointed. Although formally ministers are not involved in the recruitment procedure they are notified of the short list of candidates and the favoured option. Ministers can influence the selection by making their preferences known. Equally, ministers can influence the departmental approach in relation to its agencies. The former Secretary of State for Social Security, Tony Newton, said that Next Steps had not reduced the number of managerial issues he dealt with because of the high political profile of social security which pushes management issues into the political arena.[15] He saw that his involvement in management issues was unlikely to reduce as Next Steps develops because of the political nature of social security. The finding that the political sensitivity of an area can in effect undermine the Next Steps aims of devolvement is an important finding to which we will return in Chapter 5. The current Secretary of State, Peter Lilley is apparently taking a more 'hands-off' approach than Tony Newton. He is keen on the principles of Next Steps and on the new market testing initiative and has been involved in setting the high level targets for the agencies and in the reviews of agency performance against targets. Peter Lilley deals directly with the Benefits Agency and the other agencies are delegated to junior ministers.

Members may shape the development of Next Steps either through House debates, lobbying or by asking parliamentary questions. Chapter 6 details the extent of their activity and influence. For the purposes of this chapter however, only one point is important, that is that they have not effectively acted as a powerful influence in shaping the development of Next Steps.

The most active Select Committee has been the Treasury and Civil Service Select Committee, which has been monitoring and reporting on the development of Next Steps. The other departmental committees have, as yet, not specifically examined the development of Next Steps in their departments but have raised issues such as whether they should be shown draft agency framework documents. These committees have kept the development of Next Steps in the public eye.

The other powerful body of parliamentary scrutiny is the Public Accounts Committee which is supported by some 800 National Audit Office staff. The NAO is not a part of the civil service but has the role of authorizing and auditing government expenditures. The head of the NAO is the Comptroller and Auditor General who is an officer of the House of Commons. He has a statutory duty to certify the accounts of all government departments and a wide range of other public sector bodies and also has statutory powers to 'carry out, and report to Parliament on, examination of economy, efficiency and effectiveness in the use of resources *by those bodies he audits or to which he has rights of access*.[16]

The development of Next Steps could have important implications for the role of the NAO. At one extreme it could mean that the NAO has a smaller domain because agency functions are privatized or contracted out and it loses its access to these functions. At the other extreme it could mean that the NAO's domain expands as it becomes increasingly involved in advising agencies on their accounting arrangements, and advising departments and agencies on the selection and use of performance measures and targets. It could also expand to take on more of an active management consultancy type role, for example, by producing good practice guides. This scope for expansion has however been checked by the combination of its statutory powers and by its relations with the other Whitehall actors, notably the Treasury.

There have been some jealousies and tensions between the Treasury and the NAO in carving out areas of responsibility. An example of this relates to the advice being sought by agencies on their new accounting systems and procedures. The NAO regards advice on agency accounting systems as an area of expansion and sees itself as the main player. An NAO director summed up why the agencies come to it for advice: 'They [agencies] don't want to come to NAO for assistance but then they find that they need to. In effect, NAO advice on agency accounts is compulsory because Treasury do not want ill founded accounts that NAO will qualify'.[17]

The Treasury's view, on the other hand, is that it is the only government body giving advice not only on agency accounts but also on good practice guides and advice to departments. The NAO became more involved in developing 'alternative outputs' in the form of advice to departments and other forms of guidance but the Treasury did not like the NAO performing this function and attempted to check its activities in this direction. A further area from which NAO has been excluded has been the selection of agency performance measures and targets. The NAO do see however, that they may question the validity of a particular performance measure or of the quality of targets as a part of a value for money investigation. The NAO have not yet done this but no doubt any attempt to do so would bring them into further conflict with the Treasury.

In fact it seems that Next Steps has not helped to endear the NAO to any of the other Whitehall players. The Office of the Minister for the Civil Service effectively gave the NAO a verbal warning not to bridle the progress of Next Steps. Sir Peter Kemp gave a talk at the NAO soon after the launch of Next Steps in which he argued that the NAO should allow Next Steps to develop by not reporting on particular aspects of departments or agencies which were undergoing change. So, has the NAO been heeding Kemp's advice?

The first NAO report on Next Steps certainly set out to be uncritical and to act as a bolster to the initiative. The NAO reported in June 1989 on the arrangements for implementing Next Steps in the Office of the Minister for the Civil Service, the Treasury and five other departments: the Ministry of

Agriculture, Fisheries and Food; the Department of Health; The Department of Trade and Industry; the Department of Transport and the Department of Social Security.[18] The report clearly set out to be positive and consequently came to a positive if superficial conclusion,

> Consistent with Government's priorities for the initiative [Next Steps], the first three Agencies have been given additional financial delegations and additional responsibilities for staffing matters, including the introduction and extension of staff pay linked to performance, subject to Treasury agreement. These additional freedoms should enhance their abilities to operate independently within their policy and resources framework documents, and to achieve the more demanding financial and other performance targets that have been set for them upon their agency status. And, in the longer term, as an agency becomes more experienced in the conduct of its business, the Treasury expect it to be given further delegated powers where this is expected to deliver further improvements in value for money from the agency. If continued, the early demonstrated commitment on the part of parent and central departments to the thrust of the initiative should augur well for the success of Next Steps.[19]

Subsequent reports on the work of particular agencies have been rather more analytical, if not critical, so it seems that the watch-dog has not been entirely muzzled. For example, the NAO examined the progress of the Vehicle Inspectorate as the first executive agency and found that

> The Inspectorate have found it increasingly difficult to make the savings required to meet their targets. Although targets have been exceeded, there is a discernible downward trend in the size of the savings. It is questionable whether more large improvements can be made without further development of the Vehicle Inspectorate's agency arrangements.[20]

A further interesting point arising from this report was the fact that the NAO, who must agree on the facts in its reports with the audited body before presenting them to Parliament, had to agree its report with two bodies, the Department of Transport and the Vehicle Inspectorate. Agreeing reports has always been a long-winded task but the new dimension of having to agree the reports with both parent departments and with agencies will make the work of the NAO even more difficult as the departments and the agencies will clearly not always agree with each other. There is a danger that the NAO could become a tool in internal departmental disputes.

Conclusions

As Next Steps develops, so too does the importance of the issues about relations between the various organizational actors. Next Steps is now at a crucial stage in its development. Although, to a certain extent it has its own momentum with agencies and departments busy sorting out their respective responsibilities and developing appropriate mechanisms to support the new arrangements, this momentum would soon dry up if the Treasury were not to agree to the financial and personnel flexibilities necessary to the further development of Next Steps. Next Steps would then become another Financial Management initiative – shelved, not because of its principles but because the freedoms were not there to put the principles into practice as the Treasury becomes increasingly confident that agencies are establishing sound control and monitoring arrangements.

There are signs now however that the Treasury is being converted. It was initially cautious in allowing any financial or personnel flexibilities but is now showing signs of loosening up. This loosening up is in part a reflection of the pressure for change that has come from the Office of the Minister for the Civil Service and now from the Office of Public Service and Science. It reflects the slow alignment of the Treasury to the Next Steps principles.

Notes

1 C. Hughes (1990) *The Independent*, 31 October.
2 Efficiency Unit (1991) *Making the Most of Next Steps: The Management of Ministers' Departments and their Executive Agencies*. London, HMSO.
3 Para. 2.7, ibid.
4 Interview with senior DSS official, 8 May 1991.
5 Interview with senior DSS agency official, 3 December 1991.
6 Interview with Treasury official, 11 February 1993.
7 Interviews with Treasury officials, 11 February 1993.
8 Paras 172 and 174, *Social Security Departmental Report: The Government's expenditure plans 1993–94 to 1995–96* (1993) Cm 2213. London, HMSO.
9 Interview with Peter Kemp, 28 November 1991.
10 Quotation from senior DSS HQ official, 1 October 1991.
11 Interview with Social Security agency chief executive, 30 October 1991.
12 Interview with Child Support agency chief executive, 12 February 1992.
13 Interview with Child Support agency chief executive, 12 February 1992.
14 Interview with Benefits Agency personnel director, 26 April 1993.
15 Interview with Tony Newton, 29 January 1992.
16 National Audit Office (1987) *The Role of the NAO*. London, HMSO; (italics added).
17 Interview with NAO director, 23 March 1992.
18 National Audit Office (1989) *The Next Steps Initiative*, HC 410. London, HMSO.
19 Para. 62, ibid.
20 Para. 11, The National Audit Office (1992) *The Vehicle Inspectorate: Progress as the First Executive Agency*, HC 249. London, HMSO.

5

The move to contract government

Next Steps is about creating a series of client/contractor relationships to replace existing systems of reporting and control. The creating of a client/contractor divide for existing civil service functions involves defining who should be responsible for what and how to ensure that contractors have the freedom to get on with the job whilst being held accountable for delivering the desired ends within budget. Putting these issues another way brings us back to two of this book's main themes: how do we separate 'policy' and 'operational' issues and how do we balance autonomy and accountability? Public administration literature tells us that we cannot separate 'policy' and 'administration' and that there is a tension between autonomy and accountability.

This chapter asks whether public administration literature has been right about these issues or whether Next Steps has found a way round these dilemmas in its move to contract government. The chapter examines how Next Steps is applying the concept of 'contract government' to existing civil service functions; considers how the market testing initiative takes the move to 'contract government' a step further, from management *by* contract to the idea of management *of* contracts; and considers the implications of the changes for the development of Next Steps and for the future of the civil service.

The move to 'Management by contract'

The notion of managing or controlling by the use of 'contracts' is the backbone of Next Steps. This section considers how Next Steps is introducing 'contracts' to the civil service. It details what is in these 'contracts', how they have been working and how they have been evolving.

One of the basic principles of Next Steps is that executive agencies are provided with the freedom and the tools to get on with their 'businesses' and that in return agencies must deliver certain outputs or standards of service within the available resources. This basic principle is enforced through a series of 'contracts' which essentially specify what freedoms an agency has, how much money it has and what ends the agency must achieve. The documents forming these overall agency 'contracts' are; the agency framework documents which at present must be reviewed around every three years, the annual business plans and the three or five yearly corporate plans.

At a more detailed level, agencies contract agencies through 'service level agreements' to perform particular functions such as computer services, providing contribution record data or accommodation services. In other words, the 'contractor' becomes a 'client' organization which must manage its dealings with other contractor agencies. Individual staff are also contracted to achieve the agency aims. Agency chief executives are contracted to meet the agency targets and a proportion of their pay is dependent on them meeting those targets. The chief executives are employed on a short term basis with the renewal of their contract also being dependent on their performance. Some other senior agency staff are also employed on a short term basis and some also have their pay linked to the performance of the agency. At a lower level, the general staff of the agency are also in effect contracted to achieve the agency aims and, in recognition of this, may receive pay bonuses when targets are met.

Devising the framework documents

The framework documents, as their name suggests, define agencies' operational frameworks. All the new executive agencies have a framework document with five main ingredients: the aims and objectives of the agency; the nature of its relations with Parliament, ministers, the parent department (unless the agency is a separate department), other departments and other agencies; the agency's financial responsibilities; how performance is to be measured; the agency's delegated personnel responsibilities and the agency's role and flexibilities for pay, training and industrial relations arrangements. These framework documents must be revised at least every three years.

This section considers the process of devising the framework documents and the extent to which this explains the differences in the final documents. It then evaluates how the framework documents have been working in practice, in particular, how effective they have been in providing agencies with autonomy within a framework of accountability and how effective they have been in clearly distinguishing between 'policy' and 'operational' issues.

The process of devising the original framework documents involved lengthy negotiations between central departments, agencies and other interested parties such as the trade unions. Certainly in the cases of the Department of Social Security's Benefits Agency and Contributions Agency many trees were sacrificed in the negotiations over the framework documents wording.

The bare bones of what was to be in the framework documents were set out in guidance issues by the then Office of the Minister for the Civil Service. The early framework documents closely follow this guidance and in some instances use the same or similar forms of words, in particular, when tackling potentially difficult issues such as distinguishing between the responsibilities of ministers, departments and agencies. However, underneath some apparently similar wording is hidden some important differences in the powers of an agency. One example of this relates to the respective responsibilities of all those involved in an agency agreement – the agency itself, the department, Treasury, the Office of the Minister for the Civil Service and other agencies.

Accounting officer responsibilities

From looking at the framework documents it seems that the respective accounting officer responsibilities are a key factor in determining the theoretical nature of the relationship between all those involved in an agency agreement. Accounting officers are answerable to Parliament (and may be called to appear before parliamentary committees) for the efficient and effective use of resources within their department or agency.

The framework documents establish the accountability responsibilities of the agency chief executives. The agency chief executives are all appointed as accounting officers for their agencies. They may either be appointed by the Treasury as a second accounting officer with their own separate vote, that is where they have their own direct allocation of funding, for example, as is the chief executive of the employment service, or they may be appointed by their parent department as either an additional or second accounting officer, but not with their own votes. There is an important distinction between the two when it comes to deciding on their appropriate relationship. Both 'types' of accounting officers are responsible for the propriety of spending within their agencies, but those agency accounting officers without their own vote are only responsible for the administrative costs of running their agencies whereas second accounting officers with their own votes also have policy responsibilities.

It appears that where an agency has its own vote it also has 'policy' responsibilities. Where it does not have its own vote the Next Steps theory is the departmental headquarters accounting officer (usually the Permanent Secretary) is responsible for all 'policy' issues and the agency chief executive is responsible for the 'day to day operations' of the agency. The framework documents support this dichotomy.

On the whole, agencies with their own votes have a restricted set of policy responsibilities. For example, the Social Security Benefits and Contributions Agencies have the role of providing information and policy advice (in the case of the Contributions Agency, directly to the Secretary of State) but there is no explicit proviso that they, in turn, should be consulted about policy proposals.

The Chief Executive contributes to the Department's policy and evaluation activities by providing information on the operational implications
of current and alternative programme characteristics and by providing, to
an appropriate level of quality, such data as Ministers and the Permanent
Secretary may require to support the monitoring, evaluation and development of policy and the monitoring and forecasting of benefit
expenditure.[1]

The Agency contributes to the Department's policy development and
evaluation activities by providing information on the operational implications of current and alternative policies and by providing information to support the monitoring and forecasting of NIC collection . . .
The Chief Executive may make proposals to the Secretary of State for
changes in the policies and programmes operated by the Agency which
are designed to improve the effectiveness with which the Agency meets
its overall objectives. In doing this, the Chief Executive consults the
Permanent Secretary to ensure that any proposals submitted to the Secretary of State are consistent with the overall policy objectives of the
Department. She advises the Secretary of State of any activity which
significantly affects the Agency's ability to perform effectively.[2]

By contrast, many of the agency accounting officers without their own
votes have more limited specified roles. A number of agencies such as the
Department of Social Security's Resettlement Agency and Information Technology Services Agency have no specified role in policy development.[3] The
wording in the Resettlement Agency's framework document is fairly typical;

Department of Social Security Ministers will be responsible for determining the broad policy and framework within which the Agency will
operate. However Ministers and the Department will not normally be
involved in the day to day management of the Agency or Units.[4]

The framework documents therefore contain some variations on the
respective roles of departmental and agency accounting officers and consequently departments and agencies but by and large, often using the same words,
outline that departments remain responsible for 'policy' issues whilst agencies
should be exclusively responsible for day to day operations.

How well the agency is established

The first Employment Service framework document, like some of the other
framework documents, states that the chief executive can provide policy advice
but goes much further in specifying, 'The Chief Executive is consulted before
any policies affecting the Agency are put to the Secretary of State'.[5] This one
line is an important coup for the chief executive of the Employment Service in
terms of autonomy to manage his 'business'. It in part reflects the fact that
when Next Steps was announced the Employment Service was already fairly

well established along the path of developing as a semi-autonomous body. It was created in October 1987 from the network of unemployment offices and job centres. Indeed, Mike Fogden, the Chief Executive of the Employment Service describes Next Steps as 'an enabler which sets some parameters and provides a central push for the Employment Service in negotiating its flexibilities and freedoms'.[6]

By contrast, those agencies which were not well developed like the Child Support Agency had different aims in drafting their framework documents. For example, because the Child Support Agency is at an early stage of development its priorities are to build up an organizational structure rather than to develop its autonomy.

Respective powers in the drafting process

Returning to the Employment Service, a second reason why it was able to secure its interests in the initial framework document was because senior agency staff played a major role in drafting the framework document. In sharp contrast with other framework documents, the first Employment Service framework document was written by the department and the agency and then sent to the Office of the Minister for the Civil Service and the Treasury to be agreed. The more usual pattern was for the framework documents to be drafted by 'committee' with the Central Departments of the Office of the Minister for the Civil Service and the Treasury taking a front seat in the proceedings.

The House of Commons' Departmental Select Committees also put in their bid to play a part in drafting the framework documents in their request to see and to comment on the draft framework documents. The main problem with such an arrangement would be in deciding *which* draft should be submitted to the committees. Certainly in the case of the Department of Social Security Whitehall was true to form in the myriad of draft framework documents produced and trees sacrificed in the course of the negotiations between the various parties.

Agency funding arrangements

The degree of autonomy agencies have at their launch and the role they play in drafting framework documents have affected the amount of autonomy delegated to agencies in their first framework documents. The third factor influencing the amount of autonomy delegated to agencies in the first framework documents relates to how the agency is funded. Returning to our typology in Chapter 1, it is clear that those agencies which raise money from their goods and services and are therefore not entirely dependent on Treasury funding (for example, Her Majesty's Stationery Office (HMSO) and the Central Office of Information) were initially given more freedoms than those agencies which are entirely dependent on Treasury money such as the Social Security Benefits Agency. The reason was simple; the Treasury was reluctant to agree additional financial or personnel 'flexibilities' to agencies which may not be able to handle the new freedoms and guarantee no resulting increase in public expenditure.

In summary, drafting the initial agency framework documents has been a costly drawn out business with the final documents, in various mixes, reflecting a compromise between the interests of the Treasury, the Office of the Minister for the Civil Service, the department and the agency. The substance of the documents for example on the extent of an agency's autonomy for financial and personnel issues, also reflects the stage of an agency's development, the nature of its business and in particular whether or not it is entirely dependent on Treasury funding and most likely, its degree of political sensitivity.

Working within the framework agreements

This section considers how the framework documents have been working in practice as 'contracts' by which agencies can be 'managed' at arm's length. It focuses on two areas covered by the agency framework documents: the division of responsibilities between the various parties involved in an agency agreement and the extent to which the personnel and financial freedoms delegated to agencies in the framework documents have allowed them to get on with their jobs in the most efficient and effective way. The section then considers how the framework documents are likely to develop.

The theoretical difficulties with the division of responsibilities between departmental headquarters and agencies have been well documented.[7] The main difficulty is that despite their attempts at clarity, the framework documents fail to paint a black and white divide in respective responsibilities because of the lack of a clear dividing line between 'policy' and 'day to day operational issues'. The scope for departmental headquarters to become involved in detailed agency activities by classifying them as 'policy' is highlighted by Robert Maclennan MP who, in debating the National Audit Act stated,

> I believe that it is possible to go right through the decision making process in any Department, Authority or Body which could be subject to examination and at almost any point seek to cover the subject under investigation by the claim that it is an issue of policy . . . Policy is not determinable either as a matter of fact or as a matter of law. It can be determinable only as a matter of judgement by those called upon to distinguish it.[8]

There may be an incentive for departmental headquarters to define policy issues downwards into operational issues because ministers remain ultimately responsible for *all* of the activities of their departments and as such may be reluctant to devolve responsibility to their agencies.[9]

Classifying detailed agency activities as 'policy' provides departments with the rationale for close involvement in agency day to day affairs. This downward defining of 'policy' is more likely to happen in areas of political sensitivity such as social security. Clearly the day to day activities of the benefits agency are more likely to incite political interest than the activities of something like the Meteorological Office executive agency. For example, decisions about the layout of local social security offices are clearly operational but the questions are of considerable political interest. Should the wall to floor bullet-proof screens be removed to make the offices more friendly or would this put staff at risk? Should the offices have private areas or rooms where people can talk about their financial affairs out of the earshot of their neighbours? MPs all have social security staff and recipients in their constituencies many of whom have strong feelings about such issues.

In practice it seems that these fears have been realized. Despite the Next Steps rhetoric, as we have seen from the previous chapter, Tony Newton, when he was the Social Security Secretary of State, found that the number of managerial issues he dealt with had not reduced and he saw that the high political profile of social security meant that this was unlikely to change ('depending on the future of social security'!).

The political nature of the Social Security Benefits Agency may also explain why it was the only executive agency examined by the Treasury and Civil Service Committee in 1991 for which a departmental spokesman (a deputy secretary) accompanied the agency chief executive to the committee hearing. Indeed, Mr Montagu, the then deputy secretary who attended the hearing, was asked by the committee chairman whether he was in attendance in order to 'mind the agency'. Of course he replied that he was 'absolutely not' there to 'mind the agency'.

It does seem, therefore, that the framework documents have not been entirely successful in ensuring that the parties to an agency agreement all play their parts in ensuring the success and development of the agency. Certainly initially, some departments have been exploiting the blurred border between policy and operations in order to become more involved in agency affairs. As we have already seen, this was also the conclusion of the Prime Minister's Efficiency Unit who undertook a study in 1992, commonly known as the Fraser report, which examined the relationship between departmental head-quarters and their agencies.[10] The main thrust of the recommendations was that departments should reduce their level of involvement in agency activities.

Personnel and financial freedoms

This section considers whether the freedoms granted in the initial agency framework documents have directly resulted in changes to existing personnel and financial management practices. Overall, the initial agency framework documents have not in general granted much in the way of personnel or financial freedoms. On the personnel side, agencies were initially contracted to stay within the overall civil service pay and grading arrangements. These arrangements did allow certain flexibilities for example, to recruit staff directly but only up to relatively low levels (in most cases to clerical officer and in only seven cases out of the first 34 agencies, to lower middle management levels – grades 6 and 7) and to pay some staff group bonuses and individual performance bonuses.[11] Equally, with regard to the new financial arrangements, the first agency framework documents only allowed limited freedoms: for example, in the amounts that they could transfer between current and capital budgets, in how they could use any revenue they generate or efficiency savings they make or in the amounts or surplus they can carry between years.

This cautious start led to agencies experiencing some frustration and to some poor financial practices. For example, on the personnel side, Ros Hepplewhite, the chief executive of the Child Support Agency said that the personnel constraints meant that she was limited in her ability to match skills to jobs: 'In a market place there is a free flow of labour but if I advertise a grade 7 post, I can only have grade 7 people apply even if there are other people at more junior levels more suited to the particular post'.[12]

Equally, within the Benefits Agency, the system of assessing staff's suitability for promotion and then sending them for interviews to promotion boards without full regard to the numbers of vacancies at the more senior level available, continued throughout the early days of the agency. Again staff were not being matched to jobs. It also meant that it was difficult to keep and to motivate good staff as all the emphasis was on promotion rather than on development within a job and possibly being paid a higher salary for doing a job well.

On the financial side, there have been some examples of poor financial management resulting from the half delegation of financial freedoms. An example relates to the freedom for the Benefits Agency to carry over to the following year any underspend. At present the Benefits Agency can carry over only 0.5 per cent of its total current budget if it underspends. The incentive, contrary to the aims of Next Steps, is therefore to find ways of spending any money over and above this 0.5 per cent before the end of the financial year or it will be lost!

The initial personnel and financial freedoms as specified in the first framework documents were therefore cautious and this caution has led to some difficulties. As we have seen from Chapter 3, however, the agencies are now in the process of negotiating with their departments and with the Treasury for additional personnel flexibilities and there are also calls for greater financial flexibilities.

Developing the framework documents

This section has shown that the framework documents have not been entirely successful in structuring the relationships between the various parties involved in an agency agreement or in ensuring that agencies have the autonomy to maximize their efficiency and effectiveness. Returning to our main theme of the division between 'policy' and 'operational' issues, the failure of the Next Steps framework documents to clearly divide the responsibilities of ministers, departments and agencies and the reluctance to address this obfuscation of responsibilities suggests that administrative theory was right and that 'policy' and 'operational' issues cannot be clearly divided.

Two possible options for the future of the framework documents have been aired. As we have seen in Chapter 4, the Fraser report came up with the suggestion of 'upside down' framework documents, i.e. where the documents specify everything that an agency cannot do rather than everything that an agency can do. The idea has not entirely been laid to rest but in addition to the opposition to the idea, for example, from some Department of Social Security headquarters people, there are clearly also practical difficulties in devising a list of everything that an agency cannot not do.

The second, and most probable scenario is that the blurring of responsibilities will not be directly addressed and framework documents will increasingly fade into the background as Next Steps develops with the agency business plans becoming more important in also setting out any changes in the environment in which an agency must operate. Certainly the Department of Social Security has decided that reviewing the framework documents every three years for the very large agencies is inappropriate; 'The Secretary of State will look at the Framework Documents every three years and see if anything needs changing, but if not, the review period in which it must be revised will be much longer'.[13]

The following section looks at the agency business plans and considers how these have developed to take on this new role.

The agency business plans and corporate plans/ strategic plans

The yearly business plans set out, amongst other things, the agency's performance indicators and targets for the coming year. These plans 'contract' agencies to achieve specified targets within the specified resources and the measures are mechanisms by which central departments can ensure that agencies remain on course to meet the required ends. The future development of agencies is outlined in the annual corporate plans or strategic plans which set out the agency's agenda for the coming three or five years. The corporate/strategic plans, which are not published, are essentially the business plans combined with the predictions for the coming three to five years and the expenditure estimates.

The initial business plans were very much top down, written under the guidance of the Office of the Minister for the Civil Service by departments and senior agency staff with Treasury input. Like the agency framework documents, the business plans also go through numerous drafts which are passed back and forth between departments and agencies.

Within the Benefits Agency the system for devising the annual plans has been developing to make the plans more of a 'bottom-up' process. The aim is to move to a situation where the business plans are less of a bidding document requesting resources and more of a planning document which shows how much each section within the agency has spent in the previous year and, taking into account workloads and expected efficiency savings, how much they are likely to spend in the following year. The eventual aim is then to allocate the required resources to each of these 'sections' which will be contracted to carry out their functions within their budgets.

Agency performance measures and targets

One of the most important features of the business plan is that it sets out what the agency must achieve and the resources it will have to do this. The business plan sets out how an agency's performance is to be measured and the targets it must achieve. The experience of the Department of Social Security and its agencies indicates that deciding on what would be appropriate measures of agency performance is not a simple task. There are a number of barriers such as limitations in existing data and political sensitivities. There is also the issue of arbitration between agencies and parent departments and other central departments on the nature of the information that agencies should report.

In facing these questions and difficulties in preparing for the launch of the Information Technology Services Unit as an agency and the Contributions Unit (which was to become an agency in the following year) the Department of Social Security's branch responsible for launching the executive agencies commissioned a firm of management consultants to consult with the various parties involved and, in effect, to arbitrate on some of the issues by drawing up a proposed framework for monitoring the agencies. Table 5.1 shows the outcome from the negotiations of devising the initial performance indicators. It shows the Department of Social Security's executive agencies first performance measures and how these relate to the agency objectives.

Limitations in existing data in part explain why there are some agency objectives for which there are no performance measures. Examples where there are no performance measures for objectives relate, first, to the provision of policy advice. All the Department of Social Security's agencies have an objective relating to the provision of good quality policy advice. The main reason for the lack of performance indicators in this area is perceived difficulties of measurement. It would be possible only to devise qualitative measures, for example, by asking parent departments and/or ministers whether or not they are happy with the policy advice they have received. In New Zealand policy advice is treated as a commodity to be purchased and evaluated, just like most other aspects of the government 'business'. The quality of policy advice is routinely assessed by ministers and chief executives (heads of departments).

A second area where limitations in existing data explain why there were difficulties in devising initial agency performance measures and indicators is highlighted by the fact that there are some 'process' objectives and an even

Table 5.1   The Agencies objectives and key performance measures

---

(a) Resettlement Agency

Objective 1

'To reduce cost per person per occupied bed without loss of service'

Output	*Quantitative*	*Qualitative*
economy and efficiency	• average cost per person per occupied bed day • conduct of agency business within financial target	

Objective 2

'To establish, spread and develop best practice in resettlement units'

Process
- establish minimum sets of standards for quality of service
- to develop a methodology for defining and measuring resettlement

Objective 3

'To implement a programme for closing resettlement units'

Output	*Quantitative*	*Qualitative*
effectiveness	• closure of units	

Objective 4

'To identify and arrange staff management and staff training for resettlement agency staff'

Process
- date for implementing agency's training strategy

Objective 5

'Gain approval for RSA strategic direction for period 1992/95'

Process
- dates for developing strategy and draft business plan

Table 5.1   *Continued*

(b) Benefits Agency

Objective 1

'To develop an efficient customer-orientated benefit service, which is accessible, accurate, prompt, helpful and cost effective and which does not discriminate on the grounds of race, sex, religion or disability'

Output	*Quantitative*	*Qualitative*
economy and efficiency	• benefit clearance times • accuracy of assessments for SF, IS, INCAP, FC, WPs • remaining within budget • efficiency savings	

Output	*Quantitative*	*Qualitative*
effectiveness		• customer survey

Objective 2

'To provide comprehensive information to the public on social security benefits in accordance with guidance from the Secretary of State so that they are informed about their entitlements and enabled to claim and receive benefits; provide clear explanations of how decisions on claims are reached; and provide clear explanations of appeal and review rights'

Output	*Quantitative*	*Qualitative*
effectiveness		• customer survey

Objective 3

'Ensure that the correct amounts of benefit are paid on time with proper safeguards against fraud and abuse'

Output	*Quantitative*	*Qualitative*
economy and efficiency	• clearance times • savings from fraud work • amount of overpayment recoveries • benefit assessment accuracy	

Table 5.1   *Continued*

Objective 4

'Contribute to the Department's policy development and evaluation activities: provide information on the operational implications of current and alternative programme characteristics and to provide an appropriate level of quality, such data as Ministers and the Permanent Secretary may require to support the monitoring, evaluation and development of policy and monitoring and forecasting of benefit expenditure'

Objective 5

'Provide related services to the public on behalf of other government departments and agencies in a responsive and efficient manner'

Output	Quantitative	Qualitative
effectiveness		• customer survey

(c) ITSA

Objectives 1–3

'To maintain and operate existing computerised benefit and administrative systems and IT infrastructure, cost effectively and to specified standards of service'

'To deliver on time, to full planned functionality and within budget, the operational strategy'

'To provide computer services – including planning, project development, hardware and software systems and systems maintenance – within timescale and budget, and to specified standards of service'

Output	Quantitative	Qualitative
economy and efficiency	• to complete work programme within cash allocation • to carry out certain services within vote allocations • reduce costs – average per work hour and of chargeable hours for software development • to keep costs of paying benefits to specified figures	

Table 5.1   *Continued*

Output	Quantitative	Qualitative
Effectiveness	• the utilization of mainframe capacity • average on-line response time • average availability level	

Objectives 4 and 5

'To provide advice and guidance on opportunities to exploit current or emerging technologies in pursuance of customers' business objectives'

'To contribute to DSS's policy development and evaluation activities by providing information on the operational implications of current and alternative programme characteristics'

(d) Contributions Agency

Objective 1

'Ensuring to the maximum extent eonomically feasible, compliance in respect of national insurance contributions levied on employers, employed earners and the self-employed'

Process
• number of self-employed (class 2) contributors identified
• increase the number of surveys of national insurance contribution compliance

Output	Quantitative	Qualitative
effectiveness	• collection of contribution arrears	

Output	Quantitative	Qualitative
economy and efficiency	• complete work within budget	

Table 5.1   *Continued*

Objective 2

'Maintaining comprehensive and accuracy of individuals' national insurance contributions and credits so that benefit entitlement and rebates/incentives can be properly determined'

Output	*Quantitative*	*Qualitative*
economy and efficiency	• number of end of year returns posted by 31 December	
	• per cent of personal pension applications registered within 28 working days	

Objective 3

'Contributing to the DSS's policy development, monitoring and evaluation activities by, for example, providing information on the operational implications of current and alternative policies'

Objective 4

'Providing an accurate and responsive information service to members of the public, employers, other Government departments and agencies'

Output	*Quantitative*	*Qualitative*
economy and efficiency	• clearance time for benefit queries handled	
	• clearance time for employer, contributor and personal pension enquiries	

The Resettlement Agency objectives are from:
Department of Social Security (1991) *Resettlement Agency Business Plan 1991/92.* London, HMSO.

The Benefits Agency objectives are from:
Department of Social Security (1991) *Benefits Agency Framework Document.* London, HMSO.

The Information Technology Services Agency objectives are from:
Department of Social Security (1990) *The Information Technology Services Agency Framework Document.* London, HMSO.

The Contributions Agency objectives are from:
Department of Social Security (1991) *The Contributions Agency Framework Document.* London, HMSO.

larger number of 'process' indicators. For example, the Resettlement Agency has the process objective of identifying and establishing criteria and standards or yardsticks to measure the quality of service provided by the resettlement units. Equally, it has the 'process' objective of developing a methodology for defining and measuring resettlement. The need for this objective has arisen because at the time of agency launch, there existed only a few measures of the efficiency and effectiveness of the resettlement units. The lack of earlier measures was likely a reflection of the relatively low priority accorded by the Department of Social Security to the resettlement units.

Limitations in existing data also explain the continuing overall emphasis on quantitative efficiency indicators: 'This reflects a general weakness in the PI systems that sprang up in the wake of the FMI: the paucity of effectiveness PIs, particularly regarding any measures of quality and consumer satisfaction'.[14] It could also reflect a change in priorities. The importance of 'customer satisfaction' has increased over the last decade. Now, with Next Steps placing considerable emphasis on customer satisfaction, and with the Citizen's Charter adding its force to this emphasis, it is no surprise that limitations in existing data on customer satisfaction became an issue for many of the Department of Social Security's agencies.

The second reason why there are some agency objectives for which there are no performance measures is the political sensitivity of publicizing the current state of play. The Contributions Executive Agency has two primary objectives which are to collect national insurance contributions and to keep accurate national insurance contribution records. The agency's initial performance indicators largely measured the success of the agency in achieving the first of its objectives but there were no measures of the success of the agency in keeping accurate national insurance contribution records. There are two likely explanations. The first is highlighted by the findings of the recent National Audit Office report on the collection of national insurance contributions that indicated that the records contained a large number of errors.[15] It would be politically unacceptable to publicize widely the high proportion of inaccuracies in national insurance contribution records through new performance measures and targets. The second explanation is again limitations in existing data – there had not previously been a measure of record accuracy and it would take time to devise and set up the necessary statistical checks in order to compile such information.

In addition to the difficulties in agencies and central departments agreeing on appropriate performance measures and indicators, they faced the task of agreeing on the required standards of performance and the performance targets which the agency should meet. This creates particular difficulties where new measures have been devised and there are few indicators of what would be an acceptable level of performance. The process of target setting therefore again involved lengthy negotiations between central departments and agencies. The negotiations inevitably involved balancing the Treasury's requirement for greater efficiency savings with the Office of the Minister for the Civil Service's requirement to make Next Steps look a success by not making targets too challenging.

Since the time of these initial indicators and targets, the Department of Social Security and its agencies have been busy developing, refining and agreeing upon agency indicators and targets. One of the main reasons for these developments is that agency objectives change over time, in part, to reflect policy changes but also because they can be refined from process to output or outcome objectives. The agencies most likely to experience changing environments are those that are increasingly having to compete for work with the private sector. For example, the Information Technology Services Agency initially had a centrally allocated budget but it is now funded by customers and is increasingly having to compete with private sector bodies for its work.

Equally, as is to be expected, performance indicators and targets have been developed to adjust to the new environment. For example, the Contributions Agency had the ever-tightening target of collecting arrears of 'class 2' national insurance contributions (the contributions paid by the self-employed) but of course, the more efficient they were at achieving this target, the less the 'pot' of outstanding arrears. This made it increasingly difficult to achieve the target and consequently the target has been revised.

What is surprising is that some agencies have been going back to first principles in looking again at the ways in which they measure performance. This has been particularly true for the Benefits Agency which should, on face, have less ground work to do than other agencies. The Department of Social Security's measures and indicators go back some 20 years and are mainly related to the operations which have now passed to the Benefits Agency. The impetus for the rethink comes largely from the Citizen's Charter but it is also a reflection of the department and the agency taking the opportunity of climate of change to iron out shortcomings in existing data.

The Benefits Agency has taken a fresh look at the way in which it measures, records and reports clearance times. In looking at the measuring of clearance times it was found that different offices had been using different criteria to judge the date on which a claim was made and steps have been taken to create some uniformity in the methods used even though these could, if existing levels of performance continued, result in an increase in recorded clearance times. The agency has also taken a fresh look at the ways in which it records and reports clearance times. It has moved from average clearance times based on a sample to statements that a certain percentage will be cleared in a specified number of days (for example, 95 per cent will be cleared in five days).

In summary then, the business plans are the crucial documents in an agency agreement which 'contract' the agency to deliver certain goods or services within a certain budget. There were difficulties with developing the first business plans because of the need to develop adequate performance measures covering the main aspects of agencies' activities and because the information was not available to know what the services of each part of an agency costs. The first few years of Next Steps have witnessed a considerable amount of work in developing this information.

'Service level agreements'

A further way in which Next Steps is applying the notion of 'contract govern-ment' is in the agreements between agencies where one agency carries out a service for another. The service level agreements cut across the straight client/contractor divide as agencies who are 'contracted' to deliver certain services or goods through their framework documents and business plans become 'clients' in contracting others to perform certain services or functions.

The interconnecting functions of the Department of Social Security's agencies means that there are numerous 'service level agreements' between the different agencies. For example, the Contributions Agency provides informa-tion to the Benefits Agency on the contribution records of people who put in a claim for benefits. The Information Technology Services Agency provides computing services to all the arms of the department who have 'service level agreements' with the computing agency for each task performed. The Depart-ment of Social Security agencies' service level agreements are drawn up be-tween the agencies but with headquarters shaping the priorities within which they are framed.

Within the Department of Social Security's agencies, the aim is to move to a situation where all services are paid for by 'client' agencies. The depart-ment is in the process of developing a computer software programme which will calculate the level of charges and arrange for one account to debit another. It was not possible for money to be involved in all service level agreements from the outset because in many instances the information was not available to know the costs of particular services. There is therefore a considerable amount of work underway in developing this information.

The Department of Social Security's agencies' service level agreements have, on the whole, been viewed in a fairly favourable light by both 'clients' and 'contractors'. In particular, contractor agencies have said that they like the agreements because 'the agreements ensure that the "customer" agencies fulfil their part of the contract' and because 'they make customers more cost conscious'.[16]

An example of the agreements making customers fulfil their part of the contracts relates to the contract which the Information Technology Services Agency had to develop a departmental index. There were problems with what Information Technology Services Agency produced because the workload was far higher than the 'customers' predicted. The fact that the Information Tech-nology Services Agency had this written agreement meant that they could then show it to their 'customers' and show that the difficulties arose from the contract specifications rather than from the actual work that was done. An example of greater 'customer' consciousness also relates to the computing services. Client branches have now ceased practices such as switching on all the computers at the week-end to finish a small piece of work.

One of the main criticisms of the service level agreements is that to date there have been no penalty clauses so that if a service is not provided within the specifications, the 'client' has little in the way of recourse. The ultimate penalty clause is currently being developed in the shape of the Market Testing initiative which will take all these internal agreements one step further. The Market Testing initiative will mean that if a contractor fails to produce the goods then he is unlikely to win the contract to provide the service when it is next put to tender.

Individual staff 'contracts'

A further way in which Next Steps is introducing contracts throughout the civil service is in the form of individual staff contracts linking their pay to the performance of the agency. As we will see in Chapter 7 more staff (notably at senior levels) are being recruited to agencies on short term contracts, pay is increasingly linked to performance with the pay of senior agency staff being directly linked to the achievement of agency targets as specified in the yearly business plans, and, more generally, other agency staff may receive a group bonus if the agency meets its targets.

This chapter has therefore shown that contracts are being introduced throughout the civil service as a part of the Next Steps programme to replace existing hierarchies and lines of reporting. For example, no longer do members of agencies have direct line reporting responsibilities to more senior members of their department in headquarters. Instead, central departments manage agencies by contracts – they contract them to achieve certain ends and grant them freedoms about how they go about achieving those ends. At a lower level, agencies manage other agencies by contracts – they contract them to provide them with goods and services. And finally, staff are also increasingly managed by contracts; for example, the future employment of some senior agency staff is dependent on their agency achieving its targets.

The move to management of contract

The next stage in this development of management *by* contract is the move to management *of* contract. The market testing initiative is about putting work being done by 'contractors' within the current regime out to open competition with the private sector. This move to management of contract would not have been possible without first establishing the necessary infrastructure – the lines of distinction between 'clients' and 'contractors', the information on the costs of services and the culture and skills for 'clients' to specify their requirements. In this respect then, the market testing programme is a logical progression from Next Steps.

Implications of change

Many of the implications of this introduction of the client/contractor divide are applicable to other areas of public service delivery which have introduced quasi-markets – health, education, personal social services, housing and a number of local government services such as refuse collection. One of the most important features of these quasi-markets is the client/contractor divide with the 'client' being responsible for purchasing services and 'contractors' being responsible for providing the required service – possibly competing with other providers from either the public or private sectors for the contract. Next Steps' application of the client/contractor divide throughout the entire existing civil service and to the core of government is a major test of the structures and principles of quasi-markets in public services.

The first lesson from Next Steps is that public administration theory was right and that it is not easy to separate 'policy' and 'operational' issues, particularly in politically sensitive areas which are close to the core of government.

The second important finding from the experiences of Next Steps is that the creating of these new hierarchies and the structures to support the new arrangements does not come cheap. The transitional, periodic and permanent transaction costs are high. The devising of the contracts is a long and costly process involving large numbers of people and copious draft documents. Clearly this will be a more cumbersome process in the early days of Next Steps but it is an ongoing process as 'contracts' need to be revised and renegotiated. Information systems and reporting arrangements have also needed to be developed and this has required considerable efforts and resources, largely in the form of buying expertise from management consulting firms. Some of this work was already underway but Next Steps has its own particular needs which have required further developments and refinements. Again, much of the costs are up front or transitional but resources will continue to be required to run, maintain and refine the new systems. The aim is that Next Steps will result in a more efficient and effective civil service but any assessment of its success in achieving this aim should take into account the additional costs of the change.

Third, civil servants are being required to learn and to use different skills. The skills of drawing up contract specifications and writing tenders are relatively new to the public sector and on the whole, civil servants have had little experience in requesting tenders, writing or monitoring contracts. Equally, they have had little experience in marketing their wares and submitting proposals to compete for work. Civil servants are currently in the process of quickly acquiring these skills, with the help of management consultants. This acquisition of skills again inevitably involves costs in terms of the time and money devoted to devising, monitoring and evaluating the contracts, not least the costs of the management consultants engaged in advising departments and agencies on these activities.

A fourth effect of this move to contract government is the effect on responsiveness to environmental and policy developments. The contracts are changing the character of day to day relations and liaisons within the civil service. They require all parties to agree what is required, within what resources and by when and to stick with that commitment. 'Clients' can no longer incrementally change their requirements to match changing assumptions or priorities. Contracts reduce the flexibility to adapt to the changing environment and policy requirements. If assumptions or priorities change 'clients' must explicitly decide what to do with the original contract and possibly devise and agree new contracts.

Agencies' annual business plans establish the targets which the agencies must achieve within the specified level of resources but they make no allowance for the fact that the assumptions or priorities, on which these plans are based, may change. One example of where this has created difficulties that are now being addressed concerns the estimates underpinning the business plans. Departments' and agencies' assumptions for example on level of unemployment, inflation and rates of growth are provided by the Treasury and usually err more on the side of hopefulness than accuracy. The effect of using the Treasury assumptions in forecasting workload and developing the agencies' business plans has meant that the Benefits Agency was 'contracted' to achieve certain targets within an environment where fewer people would be claiming benefits than proved to be the case. If assumptions proved to be wrong then the agency could put in for a supplementary bid from the Treasury but this money could only come at two points in the year. The existing system was not therefore sufficiently responsive. The Treasury and the Benefits Agency are now about to introduce a system of 'workload funding' which will automatically adjust budgets (upwards or downwards) to take account of workloads.

Despite the efforts to overcome some of the difficulties of inflexibility, other obstacles are more problematic. The business plans may frustrate responsive policy innovations. The yearly contracts reduce the scope to introduce new operations within the year. This could result in operations which are less responsive to change. This will be particularly true where operations are contracted out to private bodies. These bodies will be more likely to hold departments (their clients) to rigid contracts. Also private bodies will most likely demand some longer term security of contract in order to warrant their development of an activity in a particular area.

Conclusion

This chapter has examined the Next Steps' creation of a series of 'client'/ 'contractor' divides to replace the traditional civil service hierarchy with its vertical arrangements of reporting and control. In effect there have been two stages of change. The first stage has been the move to 'management *by* contract' whereby activities are specified in a 'contract'. These 'contracts' have taken three main forms: the contracts establishing the parameters in which agencies must operate – the agency framework documents, business plans and corporate plans; the 'contracts' between departments and agencies or between agencies where one party provides a service to another – the 'service level agreements'; and the introduction of individual staff contracts such as the chief executives' contracts. The second stage of change has been the move to 'management *of* contract'. This second stage will, particularly as the Market Testing initiative develops, increasingly involve departments and agencies contracting and controlling private sector firms. To date the experience of Next Steps in developing quasi-markets has taught us two lessons. First, it has taught us that 'policy' and 'operational' issues cannot be clearly divided. Second, it has taught us that the move from hierarchy to contract is an expensive one, which, if the overall aims of achieving Next Steps are to be achieved, must continue to be offset by greater efficiency and service improvements. As we increasingly move into the next stage of reform, the stage of moving to management of contracts, two further lessons are becoming apparent. First, civil servants are having to learn new skills in developing, controlling and working to contracts. Second, the changes may reduce the ability of the civil service to be responsive to environmental and policy developments.

Notes

1 Para. 4.7, Department of Social Security (1991) *Social Security Benefits Agency Framework Document*. London, HMSO.
2 Paras 3.7 and 3.8, Department of Social Security (1990) *Contributions Agency Framework Document*. London, HMSO.
3 Para. 3.1, Department of Social Security (1989) *Resettlement Agency Framework Document*. London, HMSO; Para. 4.5.4, Department of Social Security (1990) *Information Technology Services Agency Framework Document*. London, HMSO.
4 Para. 1.5, Department of Social Security (1989) *Resettlement Agency Framework Document*. London, HMSO.
5 Para. 3.4, Department of Social Security (1990) *Employment Service Framework Document*. London, HMSO.
6 Interview with Mike Fogden, Chief Executive of the Employment Service, 27 January 1993.
7 For example, see P. Greer (1992) 'The Next Steps Initiatives: An Examination of the Agency Framework Documents', *Public Administration*, 70 (1) 89–98.
8 R. Maclennan MP, Debate on National Audit Act, 23 March 1983.
9 P. Greer (1992) op. cit.
10 Efficiency Unit (1991) *Making the Most of Next Steps: The Management of Ministers' Departments and their Executive Agencies*. London, HMSO.
11 P. Greer (1992) op. cit.
12 Interview with Ros Hepplewhite, Chief Executive of the Child Support Agency, 12 February 1992.
13 Interview with Sir Michael Partridge, Permanent Secretary, Department of Social Security, 8 February 1993.
14 N. Carter and P. Greer (1993) Evaluating Agencies: Next Steps and Performance Industries, *Public Administration*, Autumn.
15 National Audit Office (1991) *National Insurance Contributions*, HC 665, London, HMSO.
16 Group interview with ITSA managers, 30 October 1991.

6

Parliamentary and public accountability

Public and parliamentary accountability are important parts of a democratic system as they avert public service corruption and extravagance. The traditional wisdom has been that parliamentary accountability is the tool by which the British public, in theory at least, have been able to check the actions of the executive. It is about Parliament, on behalf of the public, ensuring that the executive is doing what it is supposed to be doing and is spending money in accordance with Parliament's wishes. Ministers may be asked parliamentary questions about the activities of their departments or they may be called upon to defend their departments in House debates. Ministers or senior civil servants in their capacity as departmental accounting officers may also be called as witnesses before select committees or in the case of civil servants, the Public Accounts Committee.

Next Steps and the related Citizen's Charter initiative are resulting in changes to the ways in which public and parliamentary accountability are being discharged. Next Steps faces the dilemma of how to allow autonomy within the existing framework of parliamentary accountability. As we have seen, its solution is to combine autonomy and accountability by attempting to define clearly the roles of the various parties involved in an agency agreement in the framework documents and business plans. Despite the theoretical difficulties of separating 'policy' and 'operational' issues, Next Steps aims to overcome the potential conflict between autonomy and accountability through drawing a clear distinction between 'policy' and 'operations'. Agencies are delegated the autonomy to carry out the functions they are designated and they are accountable to both central departments and directly to Parliament for carrying out these duties.

This chapter examines what changes Next Steps and the related Citizen's Charter initiative have introduced to the arrangements for securing parliamentary and public accountability and how these are working in practice.

Next Steps and parliamentary accountability

The Next Steps theory is that Next Steps will not change the fundamental principles of parliamentary accountability but will change the mechanics of how it is executed. The government's reply to the Treasury and Civil Service Select Committee sets out the aims of the new arrangements,

> The Government does not envisage that setting up Executive Agencies within Departments will result in changes to the existing constitutional arrangements . . . Establishing Executive Agencies within Departments will however involve some developments in the way in which external accountability is discharged.[1]

In other words, the theory is that the existing constitutional framework will continue to apply and that ministers will remain ultimately accountable to parliament for the activities of all of their departments. Next Steps has however, overtly introduced some changes to the mechanics of how parliamentary accountability is to be enforced with the aim of strengthening existing arrangements.

There are two main changes which Next Steps has introduced to the mechanics of how parliamentary accountability is executed. First, agency chief executives are appointed as accounting officers directly answerable to Parliament for the operations of their agencies. As the previous chapter has shown, the framework documents aim to define clearly the respective responsibilities of the new agency accounting officers, the departmental accounting officers and ministers. The Next Steps premise is essentially that ministers and departmental accounting officers are responsible for all 'policy' issues and that chief executives are accountable for the 'operations' of their agencies. Chief executives may be called as witnesses to select committee hearings and they are now responsible for answering any parliamentary questions which relate to the 'operations' of their agencies. The aim of this change is to allow Members to have more detailed replies to their questions from the chief executive who is closer to the issues than a minister who was theoretically responsible for *all* the activities of a department. The myth of the old system was that ministers were omnicompetent beings who knew everything about the operations of his or her departments.

The second change to the mechanics of parliamentary accountability results from more detailed and robust information about agencies' operations being widely available to Parliament and the public through the published agency framework documents, business plans and annual reports. The Citizen's Charter has also pushed for better information to be more generally available.

The Citizen's Charter and public accountability

The much publicized Citizen's Charter essentially aims to make the executive more directly accountable to the consumers of public services. It aims to ensure that the consumers have more information about the performance of public services. The Prime Minister, John Major makes the bold statement that it is about 'giving more power to the citizen . . . it is a testament of our belief in people's right to be informed and choose for themselves'.[2] Similarly bold, the charter itself states its aims as 'to raise quality, increase choice, secure better value, and extend accountability'.[3]

The theory behind the Citizen's Charter is that providing consumers of public services with better information about the performance of those services will increase consumers' demands for a better quality of service and thereby will result in service improvements. The Citizen's Charter, which has much wider coverage than Next Steps in that it also includes government services and utilities such as British Rail, Electricity and Gas, overlaps with Next Steps in the aim of improving the quality of service to customers of central government goods or services. Indeed, the Office of Public Service and Science regard Next Steps as 'the vehicle for the delivery of the Citizen's Charter within central Government via those Agencies which serve the public'.[4]

The theory is that the Citizen's Charter is improving the way in which external accountability is executed by introducing measures to make the executive provide the public with more information in order to make it more directly accountable to the public. As we have seen in the previous chapter, this Citizen's Charter's push for a better quality of service to the customer has encouraged public service providers to publicize the standards of service that consumers of those services can and should expect, and in some instances ensures compensation for consumers when the published standards of service are not met.

Next Steps and the Citizen's Charter are therefore resulting in more accessible and more usable information, particularly information about the performance of executive operations, being available to Parliament. For example, departmental select committees have more information on which to base their enquiries and questioning. Unlike the Public Accounts Committee, which is supported by the National Audit Office with its access to departmental records, the departmental select committees have been limited in both the extent of their resources and information and have largely depended on the information available in annual departmental reports. These departmental reports did not contain anything like the same amount of detail about departmental operations as the agency business plans and therefore the departmental select committees have less material on which to base their enquiries.

It would seem that these two main changes to the mechanics of parliamentary accountability have strengthened existing arrangements. Next Steps has however also resulted in some modifications in Parliament's powers to scrutinize the executive's activities. Some of these changes are overt reforms which are resulting from the evolving status of those agencies which are developing 'business' type accounting systems and are having some or all of their functions transferred to the private sector. Other changes are less explicitly intentional but are a consequence of the difficulties in separating 'policy' and 'operational' issues.

Explicit changes to Parliament's powers

Despite the Next Steps rhetoric that it will not affect the fundamental principles of parliamentary accountability, Next Steps and the market testing initiative explicitly introduce two main changes to Parliament's rights of scrutiny. Both of these changes are a direct consequence of agencies developing as 'business' units.

The first explicit change to Parliament's powers relates to the new agency accounting systems. An agency's accounting system is important in determining the extent of its flexibilities and freedoms. Gross accounting is basically where all receipts and expenditures are presented in the accounts and net accounting is where receipts are netted off against expenditures and only the final figures are shown. Trading funds are essentially net accounting systems operating independently of the supply system, that is, the system by which Parliament provides and receives money. As agencies develop many are changing their accounting systems from gross accounting to either net accounting or trading fund status so as to allow them greater financial flexibility to serve their new semi-autonomous status.

This increase in agency financial flexibility means a change in Parliament's methods and role in controlling agencies' finances. If an agency moves to net accounting or trading fund status then Parliament has less ability to structure how an agency should divide and use its budget and it relinquishes the right to see all of that agency's receipts. The Next Steps rhetoric is that this loss of direct Parliamentary control is balanced by departmental and treasury *strategic* controls on agency expenditure and ultimately by the requirement for the agency to balance its own books.

Contracting-out and privatization of central government activities also affect parliamentary access and therefore have implications for existing traditions of parliamentary accountability. The drive for market testing is an increasingly important change and has major implications for the development of Next Steps. Market testing is not new and indeed features throughout the 1980s but the current rigour with which market testing is being pursued, since the 1992 election, is new.

The Next Steps rhetoric always insisted it was not a precursor to privatization. Before departments establish an agency they first had to consider 'prior options', that is, whether the activities should be privatized, 'contracted-out' or not done at all. In practice, however, some activities were not ready to be privatized or 'contracted-out' but shaping them as Next Steps agencies has now made them ready. The main question is whether Next Steps did change direction. Was it originally, as it professed to be, about better management

Table 6.1   Degrees of privatization

Type 1: Privatization of management – management privatized but receiving public money and run by civil servants.

Type 2: Component privatization – contracting out of executive functions such as procurement, finance, personnel, computing services or on a larger scale of core activities such as the collection of national insurance contributions and the payment of social security benefits.

Type 3: Pure privatization – the privatization of a complete executive function or of an executive agency.

---

inside government, *or* was this a way of packaging Next Steps for the Opposition and trade unions?

Whatever the case, Market Testing and Next Steps are now closely related. They are both overseen by the Office of Public Service and Science and certainly within the Department of Social Security, there is a direct relationship between Market Testing and Next Steps. The new Minister for Social Security, Peter Lilley, is very keen on market testing and has set out three criteria that are to be used (in priority order):

1 security of supply,
2 high quality,
3 cost.

The order of priorities is worth noting as it could result in contracting-out even if it could not be justified in terms of cost. The Department of Social Security is currently running a huge market testing programme involving about 10,000 staff in both agencies and headquarters.

There are different degrees of contracting out or 'privatizing' executive activities as is broadly shown in Table 6.1.

Type 1: Privatization of management

An example of this type of privatization is the privatization of the management in the Department of Employment's Training and Enterprise Councils (TECs). They receive public money, but are managed by private businesses although they continue to be staffed by civil servants. The effect of this arrangement on parliamentary accountability has been that Parliament can continue to look at the transfer of money going to the TECs. In other words, it can question the Department of Employment about the amount which it is paying the TECs, but beyond that, Parliament has no rights of access to question the heads of the TECs about their day to day activities or the propriety of their expenditure. All it can do is refer to the TECs internal auditor's reports and accounts.

Type 2: Component privatization

'Type 2' privatization is likely to expand most as a result of the recent push for contracting-out. The Department of Social Security's Information Technology Services Agency is a good example because it competes with the private sector for a large proportion of its work. Some 70 per cent of the Information Technology Services Agency's work is now contracted-out. Other possible future examples include the privatization of the Department of Social Security's headquarters' solicitors. They are actively involved in market testing and have service level agreements for all their dealings with the department. In addition, they have already subcontracted some of their work when it has been beyond their capacity to take on the required work at a particular time. Other possibilities include the collection of national insurance contributions from the self-employed which could be carried out by a private collector, and the payment of certain social security benefits through private bodies such as banks and building societies. Moving away from social security, an obvious example of 'type 2' is the Vehicle Inspectorates and Driver and Vehicle Licensing Centre's computer service.

The effect of component privatization on parliamentary accountability is that Parliament has access to the contracts which departments draw up with the private providers but would not be able to question the providers about these activities.

Type 3: Pure privatization

An interesting example of 'type 3' privatization is the Department of Social Security's Resettlement Agency. The Resettlement Agency was established with two apparently conflicting objectives:

> to manage the facilities for temporary board and lodging provided by the Secretary of State for people without a settled way of life with the aim of influencing them to lead a more settled life;
> to implement the government's policy of closing Resettlement Units and handing over responsibility for providing alternative facilities to local authorities and voluntary organisations.[5]

The Resettlement Agency therefore has the role of 'privatizing' its functions to local authorities and voluntary bodies. As an aside, the agency has decided to transfer their remaining units as going concerns either to management through buy-outs or to local authorities or voluntary organizations, rather than closing them down as originally intended. The Department of Social Security will retain the responsibility for paying grants to those bodies which provide the resettlement services. Most likely, the department will also pursue some kind of quality control work, a regulatory function, to ensure the grants are spent appropriately. This function will probably fall to the Department of Social Security's headquarters or to the Benefits Agency and the Resettlement Agency will cease to exist.

Other possible candidates for 'type 3' privatizations include other relatively uncontroversial revenue raising agencies such as the Central Office of Information, the Queen Elizabeth II Conference Centre, the Civil Service College, the National Engineering Laboratory and the Vehicle Inspectorate. Both the National Engineering Laboratory and the Vehicle Inspectorate were earlier candidates for privatization. It seems that they are being presented again, but this time under a different guise.

If functions are completely privatized then Parliament ceases to have any rights of access or scrutiny of those functions. If however, the functions continue to receive public money, then Parliament will have the right to look at the propriety of the transfer of the money but will not be able to look at how the money is being spent.

Privatization in whatever form, therefore, removes some of Parliament's rights of access. The issue is whether this loss matters. Clearly, if it is generally accepted that a function is not a legitimate public sector function and is privatized, then this creates few difficulties. It is when the privatizations reach closer to the heart of government, for example, to some of the 'type 2' privatizations of government department services under the current contracting-out initiative, that the reduced parliamentary access to information becomes rather more contentious. For example, if the collection of national insurance contributions or the payment of social security benefits were contracted-out, then Parliament may be rather more concerned about the resulting limits on their access.

Covert changes to Parliament's powers

The covert changes to parliamentary accountability are direct results of the two tensions which are both inherent in Next Steps and which have now become familiar dilemmas – the tension between 'policy' and 'operations' and the tension between accountability and autonomy.

'Policy' and 'operations'

As we have already seen, Next Steps is founded on the assumption that 'policy' and 'operational' issues can be clearly distinguished. With regard to parliamentary accountability the theory is that ministers and permanent secretaries are accountable for all 'policy' issues and chief executives are accountable for all 'operational' issues. But, as the previous chapter also asked, how are we to distinguish between 'policy' and 'operational' issues? Does 'policy' stop at the high level of agenda setting or are the tools with which policies are implemented, the policy instruments, also to be defined as 'policy'? Equally, who is to be held accountable for ministers acting on poor quality policy advice – the ministers for taking that advice or the civil servants for providing it? Despite the attempts at clarity, under the new arrangements it is not clear who is to be held accountable for what.

As we have seen, the theoretical difficulties of dividing policy and operational issues have been well documented and yet Next Steps is apparently founded on the premiss that a clear distinction can be drawn between the two. The lack of a clear dividing line between policy and operational issues results in an obfuscation of responsibilities in the Next Steps arrangements between ministers and departmental and agency accounting officers. None of the parties know precisely where their responsibilities begin or end.

Again, the problem is not a new one. Under previous arrangements there was also some uncertainty as to the precise division of responsibilities between ministers and departmental accounting officers. The Next Steps arrangements do nothing to overcome these existing uncertainties as nowhere is there any attempt to distinguish clearly between the roles of ministers and departmental accounting officers. Indeed, the Next Steps arrangements add a further dimension to existing confusion by introducing chief executives, a further tier of players in the division of responsibilities.

In addition to the House of Commons' Committees not knowing who to call to account under the new arrangements, the National Audit Office, which serves and produces value for money reports for the Public Accounts Committee, faces additional difficulties. The National Audit Office must present agreed reports to the Public Accounts Committee, that is, the facts presented in value for money investigations must be agreed with departments. The establishment of agencies now means that the National Audit Office must agree its reports both with departments and with the agency concerned. The process of agreeing reports was previously notoriously long (and costly) and the creation of executive agencies could make the process even longer as departments and agencies may not agree with each other over certain facts.

The problem of knowing who to call to account is a particular problem in areas of political sensitivity such as social security where operational issues are more likely to reach the political agenda and ministers and permanent secretaries are more likely to become involved in agencies' detailed operations. One example where ministers have become involved in what is clearly an operational issue relates to the layout of local social security offices. Clearly the layout of social security offices and whether or not there should be glass screens and the amount of privacy required are 'operational' issues but ministers have taken an active interest in these issues because of their political sensitivity.

A further example of lack of clarity about responsibilities and accountability relates to the action taken to remedy a problem resulting from a case ruling which opened the doors for backclaims to 1948. The Department of Social Security introduced a cut-off date for backclaims with the result of creating a 'closing down sale' with thousands of applications flooding in. Headquarters' 'policy' answer to this problem was to bring forward the cut-off date to the next day, which they did without consulting the Benefits Agency. Meanwhile, without having consulted with headquarters, the Benefits Agency had come up with an 'operational' solution. They had struck a deal with the social services department concerned that all claims would be presented two days after the cut-off date for backclaims. If Parliament had wanted to know about all this, who would they have asked, the chief executive, the permanent secretary or the minister? In theory, it could either be the chief executive or the minister. The chief executive could be questioned as the issue could be defined as an operational problem or the minister could be questioned as he or she remains ultimately accountable.

Similar questions have been raised by the furore over the Next Steps arrangements for parliamentary questions. The Next Steps arrangements for parliamentary questions are that ministers answer any oral or written questions relating to 'policy' and chief executives answer any questions relating to the 'day to day operations' of their agencies. Originally ministers' questions continued to be aired in the House and published in Hansard but the chief executive's questions, answered by personal letter, were not aired in the House or published in Hansard. There are three issues here. First, in practice the new arrangements undermine the overall Next Steps premiss, set out in the government's reassurance to the Treasury and Civil Service Select Committee, that ministers would retain overall accountability: 'The further delegation of authority to managers inherent in the Next Steps concept concerns internal accountability within departments and does not conflict with the external accountability of Ministers to Parliament'.[6]

Some concern was raised notably amongst some Labour Members of Parliament such as Gerald Kaufman, Dave Nellist and Robin Maxwell and amongst academics that ministers were using the new arrangements to abdicate their responsibilities of parliamentary accountability. In a newspaper article Gerald Kaufman commented,

> Bichard [Chief Executive of the Benefits Agency] keeps writing to me, and I want him to stop. Whenever I have a constituency case involving a social security problem, I write about that case to the government minister responsible . . . Members of Parliament have no power and only two rights. One is the right of privileged speech within Parliament. The other is the right of access to ministers. We exercise those rights not for ourselves but on behalf of our constituents. If ministers seek to eliminate one of those rights, as they are doing by delegating cases to agencies, units and officials, they are diminishing the rights of our constituents and the rights of Parliament. They are diminishing democracy.[7]

This issue was taken up by the House of Commons' Select Committee on procedure which reported,

> Mr. Nellist pointed out that if a Member's question was referred to the chief executive of an agency, the resultant reply took the form of a letter which was not printed and therefore 'not available to those who consult Hansard'. Only by contacting the Public Information Office of the [House of Commons'] Library could a member of the public or interested organisation obtain a copy of the letter from the chief executive, a process described by Mr Nellist as 'enormously cumbersome'.

We share Mr. Nellist's view that this is an unsatisfactory state of affairs. We appreciate that one of the main purposes of establishing Executive Agencies was to remove their day to day operation from the direct responsibility of Ministers. Nevertheless, the fact remains that most Members expect to be able to read in the Official Report the answer to a question on a matter such as, for example, the management of local social security offices, which is of importance to their own constituents just as much as to those of the Member who happens to have tabled a question on the subject. So long as questions relating to Executive Agencies remain in order, as we trust they will, Members should be entitled to receive a reply in the normal way by written answer.[8]

The committee went on to recommend that future replies from agency chief executives in response to parliamentary questions referred to them by ministers should appear in the official report. It suggested that ministers should introduce chief executives' letters.[9] It has now been agreed that questions answered directly by chief executives will be published weekly in an appendix to Hansard but despite this agreement, these appendices have yet to be produced.

The second issue raised by the Next Steps arrangements for answering parliamentary questions again stems from the fact that it is not possible to distinguish clearly between 'policy' and 'operational' issues. The Next Steps procedures for answering parliamentary questions created the incentive for 'policy' to be defined downwards so as to prevent contentious issues from being brought to the attention of Members other than the person asking the question or to the attention of the general public. Despite this incentive, there is little evidence that many policy issues have been defined as operational issues so as to prevent such questions from appearing in Hansard. Paul Flynn MP collated chief executives' replies and published them in a monthly bulletin *Open Lines*. Analysis of the parliamentary questions which were answered by the chief executive of the Benefits Agency shows that, on the whole, the questions referred to the chief executive quite clearly related to 'operational' issues.

However, the third issue raised by the new arrangements for parliamentary questions is that the level of questions aired in the House and currently published in Hansard is being raised from the particular (Members asking parliamentary questions about the experiences of individual constituents about certain offices) to the more strategic. Table 6.2 shows the breakdown of parliamentary questions relating to the Department of Social Security in the parliamentary session 1991–92. Overall the table shows that the majority of questions were answered by the minister.

Next Steps is resulting, therefore, in some changes to the tools for ensuring parliamentary accountability. Despite government reassurances to the contrary, it seems that it is also to have some effect on the fundamental principles of parliamentary accountability. Some of these effects are probably temporary and are a reflection of the time of change but more importantly, others could have

Table 6.2 Breakdown of who answered parliamentary questions relating to social security issues between 15 April 1991 and 16 March 1992

Questions answered in full by ministers	2,118
Questions answered by Benefits Agency chief executive	189
Questions answered by other chief executives	32
Total	2,339

longer term implications. The furore over the Next Steps arrangements for dealing with parliamentary questions and some of the early mix ups over the respective responsibilities of departments and agencies are probably teething problems to be resolved. The restriction in Parliament's access, for example, to contract-out or privatize functions and the muzzling of the watch-dogs are however much more worrying.

Accountability and autonomy

The effect of the tension between accountability and autonomy on existing principles of parliamentary accountability have been evident in two areas both relating to the work of the House of Commons' committees. The select committees, the Public Accounts Committee and the National Audit Office have expanded empires and have more work than ever. In addition to their traditional tasks of securing the accountability of government departments they now have the task of securing the accountability of agencies. The National Audit Office has undertaken considerable work in advising agencies on their new accounting systems and the form of their accounts. The Treasury and Civil Service Select Committee have been particularly active in pursuing the progress and the issues raised by the Next Steps initiative. The Public Accounts Committee has also examined the progress of a number of agencies. Some of the select committees have held enquiries which have focused on the work of the new agencies. There is also more ready information to aid the committees and the National Audit Office in their work. Agencies have brought a considerable amount of literature into the public domain; there are the agency framework documents, the business plans and the annual reports.

However, Next Steps is a time of fundamental change in pursuit of the initiative's desired agency autonomy, flexibility and freedom to manage. The traditional roles of the select committees and the Public Accounts Committee, which is served by the National Audit Office, are to examine the propriety of departments' expenditures in particular areas. Particularly at the early stages of agency development, when departments and agencies are still in the stages of establishing new structures and agency corporate identities, committee reports may undermine the efforts of departments and agencies in pursuing Next Steps goals. An example is the National Audit Office report on the collection of national insurance contributions. Most of the fieldwork was completed before the Contributions Agency was established but the chief executive and the agency directors were still concerned that the report would be 'a kick in the teeth' for staff and would undermine some of the Contributions Agency's Next Steps achievements. The result is likely to be pressure particularly on the National Audit Office but also on the Public Accounts Committee and the select committees to be less critical of agencies, particularly at their early stages of development.

It is probably no coincidence that in 1991/92 the National Audit Office was subject to an external Price Waterhouse review of its approach and relations with departments. The main thrust of the report was that the National Audit Office should take a more positive and helpful approach, with departments advising on appropriate areas for investigation and the National Audit Office reporting on where departments have done something well in addition to reporting difficulties. The review also recommended that not all of the National Audit Office's value for money investigations should result in a report to the Public Accounts Committee and a Public Accounts Committee hearing. The National Audit Office is adopting most of the review's recommendations. There is a danger that the watch-dogs may lose some of their teeth.

This fear is supported by the tone of the Citizen's Charter white paper which is an intriguing document both for what it does say but also for what it doesn't say. The charter doesn't really mention parliamentary accountability or the traditional role of Members of Parliament to call public servants to account on behalf of their constituents although it does mention the National Audit Office – once, alongside the Audit Commission. The tone suggests that the primary function of the National Audit Office should be to inform the public, not parliament.

> The National Audit Office audits central government and a number of organisations which receive government funding. The Audit Commission is the principal auditor for local government and, with the National Audit Office, the NHS.
>
> Both these organisations provide a financial audit. But they also do important work in improving value for money. The National Audit Office, in its value for money studies, tends to examine aspects of individual departments in depth. The Audit Commission has specialised in comparative studies which examine value for money in the services provided by a large number of local authorities.
>
> We want to see informed, hard hitting and imaginative audit applied as widely and openly as possible. This would help the public to understand better how good and how efficient local services are. Much of the comparative information produced by the Audit Commission has helped to do this. It has given a powerful incentive to many authorities to improve performance.[10]

Equally the introduction to the Citizen's Charter talks about external accountability totally in terms of direct accountability to the consumer rather than through parliamentary representation.

In a free market, competing firms must strive to satisfy their customers, or they will not prosper. Where choice and competition are limited, consumers cannot as easily or effectively make their views count. In many public services, therefore, we need to increase both choice and competition where we can; but we also need to develop other ways of ensuring good standards of service.[11]

The combination of the changes to Parliament's powers resulting from the Next Steps initiative and the Citizen's Charter's efforts to increase consumer power is pushing the balance of external accountability from parliamentary to direct public accountability.

Members' interest in changes

One key factor in ensuring that parliamentary accountability is upheld particularly in a climate of change is the extent of parliamentary interest in the changes. One indicator of this is the number of MPs asking parliamentary questions about the changes. Table 6.3 outlines percentages of Members asking parliamentary questions, between 1988 (when Next Steps was launched) and 23 May 1991, relating to the development of Next Steps. (It excludes questions about detailed agency operations which were answered by personal letter from the chief executive.) Table 6.3 shows that interest was fairly high with one in 10 Members asking something about Next Steps. This interest will at least have acted to keep Next Steps on the political agenda and to keep its development in check.

The picture becomes even more interesting when we consider which Members of Parliament have been most involved in asking questions about the development of Next Steps (Table 6.4). Many of these Members also have other hats. Who is John McAllion? He is Labour Member for Dundee East but more importantly he is the National Union of Civil and Public Servants' (NUCPS) Parliamentary Consultant. Tim Smith is Parliamentary Consultant for Price Waterhouse; John Garrett, Graham Allen and Dale Cambell-Savours are or were members of the Public Accounts Committee or of the Treasury and Civil Service Select Committee and John Marek was the opposition spokesman on Treasury matters.

Table 6.3 Percentage of Members of Parliament asking parliamentary questions on Next Steps between 1988 and 23 May 1991

	%
Any question	11
On civil service terms	4
Process of establishing agencies	4
Effect on parliamentary accountability	2
Privatization	1

Table 6.4   Number of parliamentary questions asked by Members of Parliament (five or more questions)

John McAllion	47
Tim Smith	13
John Marek	8
John Garrett	7
Graham Allen	6
Dale Cambell-Savours	5
Jim Cousins	5
Bruce Grocott	5

Conclusions

Next Steps blurring of responsibilities between those accountable to Parliament is not a new problem but Next Steps apparently scientific approach to defining responsibilities has resulted in adding a further tier to existing confusions. Despite government reassurances that it attaches 'great importance to the continued full accountability of Ministers to Parliament for the whole of their Departments, including Agencies',[12] this chapter has shown that Next Steps indirectly and directly affects both the ways in which parliamentary accountability is upheld and the fundamental principles of parliamentary accountability. First, Next Steps overtly creates new structures for upholding the traditional principles of parliamentary accountability with agency chief executives being appointed as accounting officers, directly accountable to Parliament for the day to day operations of their agencies. Second however, early difficulties with the new structures created the scope for 'unintentional' changes to parliamentary accountability. For example, ministers had the scope to define contentious parliamentary questions as operational issues so as to prevent such questions from being aired in the House or published in Hansard. Third, the fundamental principles of parliamentary accountability are being challenged by privatizations and in particular, the recent drive for market testing and contracting-out. It could be argued that there is no problem, as the newly privatized functions, possibly controlled by government contracts, are not legitimate roles of government and so Parliament should not have access to them. Parliament does not have direct access to the BBC or to the electricity companies so why should it have direct access to the activities of a privatized agency such as the National Engineering Laboratory? The National Engineering Laboratory or other 'consultancy' or 'production' type agencies create few difficulties. However, as the market testing programme develops we may be applying the same issues to agencies or parts of agencies close to the heart of government, such as social security. Once the programme has developed to this stage the fact that contracting-out or privatization restricts parliamentary access will most likely raise more concerns.

This chapter has shown that there is a move away from parliamentary powers to direct public powers to secure the accountability of public service providers through the Citizen's Charter. The Citizen's Charter can supplement parliamentary accountability in so far as standards of service but it cannot replace it. The public do not have the organization, possibly the technical expertise or the teeth of Parliament to call public spenders and service providers to account.

Notes

1 The government reply to the Eighth Report from the Treasury and Civil Service Committee (1988) Session 1987–88, *Civil Service Management Report: The Next Steps*, Cm 524. November, London, HMSO.
2 Foreword (1991) *The Citizen's Charter*, Cm 1599. July, London, HMSO.
3 *The Citizen's Charter* ibid.
4 Para. 29, *Next Steps Briefing note* (1992) Office for the Public Service and Science, December.
5 Department of Social Security *Resettlement Agency Framework Document* (1989) Unpublished document. London, HMSO.
6 The government reply to the Eighth Report from the Treasury and Civil Service Committee (1988) op. cit.
7 G. Kaufman (1992) 'Privatising the Ministers', *The Guardian*, 7 December.
8 Paras 122 and 123, House of Commons Select Committee on Procedure, Third Report *Parliamentary Questions*, HC 178. May, London, HMSO.
9 Para. 124, House of Commons Select Committee on Procedure ibid.
10 *The Citizen's Charter: Raising the Standard*, Cm 1599. (1992) July, London, HMSO, p. 37.
11 *The Citizen's Charter*. op. cit., p. 4.
12 *The Next Steps Initiative: The Government reply to the Seventh Report from the Treasury and Civil Service Committee (1991) Session 1990–91*, HC 496, Cm 1761. November, London, HMSO.

7

The changing civil service

For our ethos is easy to crack:
With no contract, we can't get the sack,
We fear no election;
We've pension protection,
And there's always the Crown at our back.[1]

Next Steps and the related Market Testing initiative are transforming the British civil service and this transformation has implications both for the future organization and traditions of the civil service and for its constitutional role as a politically neutral instrument serving Parliament. The creation of executive agencies from the operational arms of government, the delegation of freedoms to these agencies to organize themselves in ways most suited to meet their 'business' needs and the possible contracting-out of existing civil service functions is indeed a 'revolution' in terms of the future development of the civil service and its role.

This chapter considers the implications of the Next Steps and Market Testing changes for the future organization and traditions of the civil service and then considers the wider implications of these changes for the future of the civil service and for its constitutional role.

The divide between 'policy' and 'operational' people

One of the main things that is changing are civil servants' working environments and the nature of their day to day jobs. The characterizing feature of Next Steps, the creation of executive agencies from the 'operational' arms of government, reinstigates the policy versus administration cultural and skill divide which Fulton tried so hard to remove. The structure of Next Steps formalizes the divide between the 'operational' agency people and the 'policy' people in headquarters. This structural reform has required agencies and headquarters to organize themselves so that they have distinct organizational hierarchies and in some cases, in the light of experience, to reorganize themselves again to best suit their new roles and 'business needs'. For example, the Information Technology Services Agency experienced 'considerable movement and reorganization in its top management structure because the structure was pretty well set up from scratch and has inevitably been revised in the light of experience'.[2]

Some agencies had more work to do than others at the outset to develop distinct organizational structures. Those agencies which already operated either as distinct branches of departments or indeed as separate departments (such as HMSO) clearly had less work to do in developing the essential ingredients: complete organizational structures, management and financial management information systems and distinct organizational identities with which staff relate. Other agencies had considerably more work to do. The close relationship and interdependency between the various arms of the Department of Social Security meant that its agencies had considerable work to do in developing organizational structures.

Next Steps also required departmental headquarters to consider their roles and to reorganize themselves. As Chapter 3 has shown, the Department of Social Security headquarters has defined its main functions and reorganized itself in recognition of its evolving roles. This structural divide encourages agency and headquarters staff to apply and develop different skills and consequently to develop different outlooks.

Agency civil servants are being encouraged to be more innovative and pro-active rather than reactive and indeed are being financially rewarded for coming up with ideas and actions to develop the work of the agencies in accordance with their overall aims. For example, the Vehicle Inspectorate Executive Agency introduced Saturday testing of vehicles in its attempt to make its services more accessible and the social security Benefits Agency is currently thinking about whether it could sell some of its training courses to local authorities. By contrast, headquarters people, particularly in finance departments, retain their primary concerns with costs and propriety and have little to encourage them to be innovative.

Although, at least within the Department of Social Security, there is a slight unease at this separation going too far and there are plans for those on the fast stream career paths to spend at least some time in agencies as a stage in their career development, any movement between headquarters and agencies or between agencies within a department will become more difficult as agencies are increasingly delegated additional freedoms. The separation of 'types' of people within headquarters and agencies is likely to become more entrenched as agencies develop and are allowed more freedom to organize their pay and grading structures and recruitment and promotion practices to suit their own requirements.

Existing civil service uniformity

Although the civil service has been characterized by a certain diversity in the range of functions performed by the different branches, based in very different settings, there has been a high degree of uniformity in departments' hierarchies, terms and conditions of employment and traditions. The delegation of freedom to agencies to organize themselves in the way best suited to their 'business needs' is increasing diversity. Increased diversity is a direct intention of Next Steps. The original Efficiency Unit report which launched the initiative saw that

> the advantages which a unified Civil Service are intended to bring are seen as outweighed by the practical disadvantages . . . the uniformity of grading frequently inhibits effective management and . . . the concept of a career in a unified Civil Service has little relevance for most civil servants.[3]

Pay and grading

Next Steps is introducing two main changes to existing pay and grading arrangements. First, it is encouraging agencies to use the scope for bonuses and performance pay within existing civil service pay agreements to motivate their staff and second, agencies are increasingly being granted the freedom to break entirely from existing civil service pay and grading structures and to negotiate with the Treasury in establishing their own arrangements (see Chapter 4, pp. 50–51). These changes are increasing the diversity in arrangements between the different parts of the civil service and are making it more difficult to move between its different arms.

As noted earlier, the Next Steps aim is to encourage agencies to be more efficient through paying financial incentives to staff such as group bonuses if agencies meet their targets and individual performance bonuses. In addition, senior agency staff have their pay linked to the achievement of agency targets. This use of incentives has been creating differences in the employment packages available to staff who used to work side by side as a part of the same organization. For example, the Department of Social Security's Information Technology Services Agency staff received a group bonus (of about £40 each) in the first year of its operation whereas no such bonus was available to the staff who came under the management of the Benefits Agency. More importantly however, agencies are increasingly being granted the freedom to bargain for their own pay and grading structures. This freedom will provide agencies with considerable scope to move away from centrally determined arrangements toward different ways of organizing themselves.

The way in which agencies bargain for their own pay and grading structures has evolved since the early days of Next Steps. Originally, the Treasury's approach was to ensure that agencies had watertight financial bases for changes to their pay and grading structures. More recently, the Treasury states that its starting premiss is that change is normal and, if there is a better way of doing something, agencies should be encouraged to follow this path. Agencies still must provide a business case which demonstrates the improvements which the change is expected to bring about.

The original system was that agencies came up with a package which consisted of job evaluations of the people in their agencies and supporting decisions on how much those people should be paid. These submissions to the Treasury had to be accompanied by an evaluation of where savings could come from to offset any immediate costs arising from the introduction of the new pay and grading package. An example of an agency which did bring in new pay arrangements under this regime was HMSO which, since October 1990, pays its staff on average 5 per cent more on the understanding that financial productivity would increase and the increase in the salary bill from increased earnings would be offset by staff savings. Few other agencies were successful in negotiations for pay and grading arrangements and even for those that were, the negotiations were long winded. The HMSO negotiations took two years even though HMSO was in a strong position because it had been operating as a trading fund for a number of years and had a good track record.

The system of the day was not working. The Next Steps aim of increasing delegation was being frustrated by the lack of success of most agencies in negotiating any agreements for additional pay and grading flexibilities. The Treasury has now changed its tactics. This is in part because of a recognition by the Office of the Minister for the Civil Service and by the Treasury that things were not working. The Office of the Minister for the Civil Service put pressure on the Treasury to relax existing arrangements and the Treasury was willing to do this because it was now more confident with the controls for monitoring the activities of the new agencies. The Treasury therefore stated that it is taking a more pro-active role because 'it is consistent with the philosophy of Next Steps and, it [the Treasury] wanted to allow more freedom'.[4] It also saw that it would result in a more cost efficient use of the pay bill and better value for money because it would help the way in which departments and agencies are run.

The Civil Service Management Functions Act was passed in 1992 which eased restrictions on what delegations could be made to agencies. From April 1994 the largest agencies will take on their own pay bargaining, including the Department of Social Security's Benefits Agency, Information Technology Services Agency and the Contributions Agency.

The Treasury do not have a set pattern for whether they will negotiate with departmental headquarters, directly with agencies or with both. The Treasury informed me however that they would not be prepared to agree to changes to an agency's pay and grading arrangements if they were the subject of a dispute between the agency and the department. The Treasury states that it would expect such disputes to be resolved before it was approached. The Department of Social Security's headquarters is much of the view that the department and its agencies must operate as a 'single department' so it is likely that it will continue to be the department negotiating with the Treasury on the agencies' behalf. One of the concerns of the Department of Social Security's headquarters is that there should continue to be parity in the pay and grading arrangements between its own agencies. This parity would ensure that staff could still be moved between the department's agencies with a minimum of difficulty. More importantly, it ensures that staff in the smaller agencies with less bargaining power and scope for efficiency savings do not become the poor relations of the larger agencies, with their staff being paid less.

On the whole agencies are in the relatively early stages of negotiating their own pay and grading structures and are still at the stage of addressing sensitive issues about which staff are more marketable and valuable and should be paid more and which are more dispensable. But once these delegations are further down the track they will raise the scope for considerable divergence from existing civil service commission arrangements so long as agencies remain within their cost/benefit analysis projections of pay and grading which they presented to the Treasury. The scope for moving away from uniform civil service arrangements will be further increased if agencies are allowed to use a proportion of their efficiency savings in the salaries budget.

Recruitment

This increasing diversity between the different arms of the civil service has also been accelerated by the revised arrangements for recruitment. There have been two main changes to existing recruitment arrangements: agencies have increased powers to recruit directly the staff they require and short term appointments are increasingly being used to recruit people externally to senior civil service appointments.

The power of an agency to recruit up to a specified level directly breaks the levelling influence of the civil service commission in decisions on the type of skills and characteristics that are desirable across the breadth of the civil service. This freedom for an agency to recruit (and train) the 'type' of staff it requires in terms of (specialist) skills and personalities could lead to an increasing divergence in staff characteristics between agencies and between agencies and departmental headquarters. The new Child Support Agency has recently been carrying out its own recruitment and has had some freedom to seek people with particular skills, although this freedom has been limited by the fact that the new agency has had to recruit most of its staff from other Department of Social Security agencies needing to shed staff. At present, certainly within the Department of Social Security's agencies, most posts have to be (usually internally) advertised at a particular level, for example, grade 7, and only people either currently working at that grade or who have been promoted to that grade may apply. This is changing, however, particularly as more posts are being opened up to people from outside the civil service.

This leads us to the second change to existing recruitment practices, the increased use of short term appointments, particularly at senior levels, which appears to be having a more consequential effect on the traditional civil service. All chief executives, both internally and externally appointed, are on short term contracts as are many other of the senior agency staff. The arrangements vary between agencies and have been developing over time. More posts are now being externally advertised and even if a chief executive's performance has been satisfactory, his or her post may be externally advertised at the end of the contract and the chief executive may have to apply for his or her own job. This happened to Mike Fogden, the chief executive of the Employment Services agency who did retain his job but said that the process was 'by no means a walk-over'.[5]

Before being appointed as chief executive of the Employment Service when it became an executive agency, Mike Fogden was in effect already doing the job and so was an internal candidate. On the whole, chief executives who were internal candidates for the job have the choice of sacrificing their civil service privileges, notably their rights to membership of the civil service pension scheme and to 'tenure'. If they sacrifice these privileges they are able to earn more in performance bonuses whereas if they retain them they have a reduced capacity to earn these bonuses. Chief executives without 'tenure' can earn up to 20 per cent of their pay in performance bonuses whereas those with tenure and pension rights can only earn up to 5 per cent. Many of the internal candidates have chosen to retain their civil service privileges (mainly because of their age and their pension entitlements).

Again returning to the example of Mike Fogden, the chief executive of the Employment Service, he did not sacrifice his 'tenure' for higher performance bonuses but said that the security this gave him was only notional as it was outlined by 'some woolly wording in my contract about another job being found for me in the civil service if a suitable appointment were available'.[6] Clearly the issue of what to do with those chief executives who were internal candidates but who are not to remain in post at the end of the contracted period is a difficult one. There are likely to be difficulties of readjustment if they are offered alternative appointments within the civil service.

The implications of this increasing use of short term contracts for senior posts and the rise in direct recruitment from outside the civil service are twofold. First, the direct recruitment from outside will clearly change the characteristics of those dominating the senior civil service posts within the agencies and possibly ultimately within departmental headquarters. Second, it will change the career patterns and promotion expectations of aspiring civil servants. The other effect will be to reduce the extent of movement between different arms of the civil service. This latter point was made by Sir Peter Kemp (the former civil servant responsible for implementing Next Steps) when he outlined the Next Steps plan: 'to extend the use of period appointments and to reduce the extent of movement within the civil service'.[7]

At present the direct recruitment of people to senior levels from outside the civil service has been concentrated within the executive agencies. This has meant that the 'new blood' has all gone into the agencies whilst departmental headquarters are still run by 'old blooded' civil servants. For example, the Department of Social Security's Benefits Agency has 'outsiders' holding its key posts – the chief executive and the finance director (the finance director's number two has also come from outside the service).

As Next Steps has effectively created a two way flow of people in and out of the civil service it also follows that the most effective way to top posts may not necessarily be to join the service as a fast stream graduate or as a direct entrant grade 7 and to follow the traditional service fast stream career route. Chief executives are being recruited to levels as high as grade 2 (deputy secretary) and it follows that existing high grade civil servants, who may have had their ideas of promotion quashed by such an external recruitment, may increasingly look beyond the perimeter fence of the civil service for their next move.

In summary then, Next Steps is increasingly changing existing uniformity between departments and agencies and these changes have implications for the degree of movement between the different arms of the civil service and for the idea of the civil service as a career job for life.

Civil service job security

A further factor which is affecting the notion of the civil service as a secure career is the fact that it no longer guarantees a job for life. Indeed, Sir Peter Kemp, the former head of the Next Steps unit, outlined the Next Steps aim: 'to encourage civil servants to build their own careers and to move in and out of the civil service'.[8] It has been no secret that one of the desires of the current Conservative Government has been to reduce the size of the public sector and equally, it is no secret that Next Steps and the Market Testing programme will serve this desire.

Table 7.1 shows how the number of civil servants has declined by nearly a quarter since the beginning of the present Conservative Government's first term of office from 733,176 in 1979 to 562,388 in 1990. These statistics mainly reflect the various mergers, divides and transfers of functions from the civil

Table 7.1   The size of the civil service

Year	Number of civil servants in post	Percentage of 1979 figure
1979	733,176	100
1980	707,620	97
1981	695,070	95
1982	675,424	92
1983	652,534	89
1984	623,972	85
1985	599,026	82
1986	594,365	81
1987	597,814	82
1988	579,627	79
1989	569,215	78
1990	562,388	77

Source: Adapted from the civil service statistics.

service to elsewhere, including non-departmental public bodies, Public Limited Corporations (for example, the Royal Ordnance Factories), and other bodies (responsibility for the Department of Health's special hospitals was transferred to health authorities). We will now however increasingly witness real reductions as the Next Steps and Market Testing programmes mature. The combination of Next Steps restructuring to increase efficiency coupled with the increasing contracting-out of existing civil service functions under the Market Testing programme, all against a background of other environmental changes such as the development of technology, will increasingly require both voluntary and compulsory redundancies.

Learning to deal with 'management by/of contracts'

A further main change to the work of the civil servant is that the nature of their jobs is changing to be increasingly dominated by 'contracts'. As Chapter 5 documented, civil servants are now engaged in a series of contractual relations, at some points as the contractor (the client) and at others as the contracted (the contractor). As we have also seen this requires them to learn new skills in drawing up tenders, proposals, contracts and in working to contracts which will change. Furthermore, the move to contracts is changing the way in which the civil service operates including its flexibility and responsiveness to respond to policy or to other environmental developments.

Implications for the future of the civil service

The changes outlined above have some important implications for the future of the civil service. First, the service is clearly going to be much smaller and more diverse. The term 'civil servant' will become increasingly meaningless and people will instead identify more with their particular role, for example as an employee of a particular agency. Although the changes to date have primarily affected those civil servants in agencies, the headquarters' mandarin class will not remain entirely unscathed. As we have seen their expectations for promotion may be undermined by those coming into agencies at senior levels who may move on to take posts in headquarters and there may soon be some direct appointments at senior levels within headquarters.

The civil service will largely be concerned with contracting, controlling and, at least initially, competing for contracts. Clearly, once civil servants have lost a tender to carry out a particular function it is unlikely that they will continue to be around to compete when the contract next comes up for competition. Departmental headquarters are currently involved in 'contracting' as 'clients' for agency services and increasingly may be involved in 'contracting' as a 'contractor' for example, if headquarters are 'contracted' (by ministers?) to provide certain services such as the provision of policy advice.

The changes have profound implications for the renowned civil service characteristics of security and loyalty. More people will be moving in and out of the civil service at all levels and there will be less job security. This may erode the 'public service ethos' where people profess to be willing to work for less money than they could command outside in return for their job security and satisfaction.

Implications for the constitutional role of the civil service

The role of the civil service in the British political system is renowned for two main features: its political neutrality and its anaesthetizing influence on radical reform. The Next Steps changes raise questions about both of these features.

The characteristic political neutrality of civil servants could be threatened if the appointment of people from outside the civil service to senior posts on a contract basis also developed to apply to headquarters posts. Although formally ministers are not currently directly involved in making the decisions on who should or should not be appointed, they are informally asked for their opinions of the short list of candidates and can therefore influence the choice. Clearly there is a danger that each change in government could be accompanied by a change in senior civil servants, as and when the contracts come up for renewal. Also, Next Steps may change the nature of the relationship between civil servants and ministers as those civil servants on short term appointments may be more committed to the task of pleasing their ministers than to servicing the civil service traditions.

The wish to please may also reduce the anaesthetizing effect of the civil service on radical reform. Senior civil servants and chief executives on short term contracts will be anxious to make an impression during their contracted years with the consequence of increasing dynamism, willingness to move with the times and to please.

The other factor which may reduce the anaesthetic is the increased infiltration of the civil service by the ideas of people from other walks of life. This infiltration is likely to make the civil service increasingly pro-active and less resistant to change. As we have seen external recruits are being directly appointed to senior civil service posts and also importantly, management consultants are increasingly used to carry out both discrete blocks of work (for example in 'managing the change or in developing information or personnel strategies) and to work alongside existing staff for example in the Information Technology Services Agency, to offset any short term difficulties of understaffing. People with experience of business, the city and industry have been appointed as advisers on departments' and agencies' boards. These 'outside' influences are changing the culture of the service to more of 'why not?' rather than 'why?'

This change will make it easier for government to implement policies directly with little civil service resistance or distortion. In turn this has considerable implications both for the new relationship between governments and the civil service and for what governments are able to achieve.

Notes

1 Verse from a senior civil servant in the early days of Next Steps, 1 October 1991.
2 Quotation from group interview with Information Technology Services Agency Management team, 30 October 1991.
3 Para. 11, Efficiency Unit (1988) *Improving Management in Government: The Next Steps*. London, HMSO.
4 Interview with Treasury official, 11 February 1993.
5 Interview with Mike Fogden, chief executive of the Employment Services Agency, 27 January 1993.
6 Interview with Mike Fogden, 27 January 1993.
7 Interview with Peter Kemp, 28 November 1991.
8 Ibid.

8

Public service reform in New Zealand and Canada

The experiences of other countries can enable us to answer some important questions about central government reform. The current drive to improve management in government and to increase efficiency, effectiveness and quality of service to the customer is common to many developed countries. The aim of this chapter is to see what the experiences of other countries tell us about Next Steps. It takes as its examples Canada and New Zealand as they are both based on the Westminster model with its conventions of ministerial responsibility. They have also both taken different directions of reform to each other and to Britain but all along the 'new public management' route. Their reform initiatives have similar aims and objectives but some important differences.

The aim of the chapter is not to evaluate the reforms of Canada and New Zealand but rather to draw on their experiences to explore whether some of the dilemmas inherent in Next Steps (such as the problems of distinguishing policy and operational issues and balancing accountability and autonomy) have been overcome by other countries' initiatives. The chapter also addresses the question of why, when there are a number of similarities in the conditions prompting reform, that the three countries should adopt different initiatives. Is there something unique to Britain to make it take the Next Steps route?

The Canadian reforms

There are some parallels between the British, Canadian and New Zealand environments in which their respective initiatives were launched. The overriding environmental factor dominating Canadian public policy has been the fiscal crisis which began in 1984. This fiscal crisis coupled with a poor opinion of the generally unpopular public service concentrated attention on ways of reducing public expenditure through policy changes such as restricting entitlement to social welfare benefits and through managerial and personnel changes including the freezing of public sector staffing and pay.

Such a background provided fertile ground for public service reform and the development of Canada's Public Service 2000 initiative. Unlike the British Next Steps initiative however, the Canadian reforms are about concentrating on existing institutions rather than about introducing new types of institutional changes. The rationale for this is that the Canadian public service went through enormous structural change in the 1970s and now only needs an overhaul, a streamlining of internal machinery and a catalyst to change attitudes inside the organization.

The Public Service 2000 initiative

The Canadian Public Service 2000 initiative was announced by the Prime Minister of the time, Brian Mulroney, in December 1989. Its aim is to 'renew the Public Service of Canada' to 'enable the Public Service to provide the best possible service to Canadians into the 21st century'.[1] Wherever the aims of the Public Service 2000 initiative are outlined, the emphasis is very strongly on improving service to the public. Indeed, a government briefing note outlined the aim as being 'to make the federal public service a client-orientated organisation . . . to ensure that we are organised, recruited, assigned, trained, and motivated towards *Service to the Public*'.[2]

On announcing Public Service 2000, the Prime Minister outlined some of the areas where changes would be made. He said that:

- the government's employment and personnel management regime will be made less complicated and burdensome for managers and employees alike;
- central administrative controls will be reduced so as to give Deputy Ministers [Public Servants heading departments] greater freedom to manage their departments and clearer accountability for results;
- the roles of central agencies and of systems of personnel and administrative control throughout the government will be clarified and simplified; and
- innovative ways to encourage efficiency and improve programme delivery will be developed.[3]

On face then, Canada's Public Service 2000 initiative looks very similar to Next Steps – its aims are to improve efficiency and quality of service and this is to be achieved through rationalizing existing procedures, allowing 'greater freedom to manage' and through refashioning existing accountability arrangements. Despite these similarities in aims however there are some important differences both in the process of implementing the respective initiatives and in their substance.

The Canadian process of reform

The Canadian reform process is characterized by extensive review and consultation. The rationale for these reviews and discussions is explained by John Edwards, the Public Servant Managing the Public Service 2000 secretariat, who argues 'the reforms are 70 per cent about attitudinal change, 20 per cent about changes in systems and processes and 10 per cent about legislative change'.[4]

The first stage of reform under the Public Service 2000 initiative was to form 10 'task forces', each assigned to report on an area where changes were required to 'renew the public service of Canada'. The people on the task forces included senior departmental staff deputy ministers (the public servants heading departments), assistant deputy ministers and senior regional officials. The task force members talked to people in their own departments for their ideas on how things could be changed and surveyed the views of thousands of public service employees. The task forces each then produced detailed reports of their findings and some 300 recommendations for the future of the public service. Table 8.1 outlines the some of the main recommendations of the task forces.

Table 8.1   Some of the main recommendations of the task forces

---

Consultation and service
- The public service must make consultation a standard operating responsibility.
- There must be more efforts to strengthen relations between the private and public sectors such as more personnel exchange programmes.

Corporate culture and service
- The task force made several recommendations for a reorientation of the public service towards service.

Monitoring service to the public
- The task force recommended that departments institute monitoring practices linked to specified acceptable standards of service designed with the involvement of front-line staff.

Information technology and better service
- Departments must use new technology in the wider context of setting new goals and in improving the quality of service.

Improving public service
- Improvement must be pursued in the context of a basic reshaping of the organization's culture into a reoccupation with client services.
- The public service must become more accessible and visible, one that engages the public in the decision making process.

Source: Treasury Board of Canada (1990) *PS2000: Summaries of the Reports of the Task Forces*. Ottawa, Ministry of Supply and Services. August.

The task forces' recommendations were reported to public servants and formed the basis of a series of discussions. A year after the task forces had reported, the Prime Minister issued the white paper outlining plans for reform.[5] The main thrust of the Canadian white paper is very different from that of the Next Steps initiative. The emphasis of the Canadian white paper is weighted to present the public service as being an emblem of national pride with the recommendations for reform (which do not begin until page 62) being very much about

> streamlining and institutional simplification [which] can be achieved without sacrificing, or in any way calling into question, the professional and non-partisan character of the Public Service, which is fundamental to the integrity and credibility of these reforms.[6]

Again this shows that Public Service 2000 is very much about reforming within and strengthening the public service and is not (neither explicitly nor it seems implicitly) about contracting-out and privatization.

The white paper recommendations fall under four headings: 'service to Canada and Canadians', 'careers within the public service', 'a more people orientated public service' and 'accountability'. Many of these recommendations are about delegating more freedoms to departments for example, to manage their budgets and buy capital items, to manage their staff and to recruit casual employees. Unlike in Britain, these powers were all held by the Treasury Board. Also, unlike Britain, Canada has a written constitution and much of its public service is governed by legislation. The new delegations as outlined in the white paper therefore have required legislative change, for example, to the Finance and Administration Act, the Public Service Employment Act and the Public Service Staff Relations Act. This requirement for legislative change has inevitably slowed down the process of reform mainly because it takes a considerable length of time to get a slot for Parliament to consider the legislative changes.

The Public Service 2000 initiative is therefore a centrally led reform which is essentially about delegating departments more responsibility and freedoms from central controls with the aims of improving service to the public, the working environment for public service employees and improving accountability arrangements.

The Canadian special operating agencies

In addition, as a part of the programme of reform, 15 special operating agencies have been established as an 'experiment'. They are mainly bodies that charge for their services and are likely to be privatized such as the Canadian Communications Group (whose role is rather like HMSO). They are being set up very much as a part of their departments and unlike the British executive agencies, the heads of the special operating agencies are answerable to senior members of their departments as their line managers. Also unlike the UK executive agencies, the heads of the Canadian special operating agencies are not directly accountable to Parliament for the agencies' activities. The departmental

deputy minister and the minister remain constitutionally responsible for reporting to Parliament (although in practice, agency chief executives have also been
asked to attend House of Commons committee hearings).

The manager of the Public Service 2000 initiative, John Edwards, described the special operating agencies as 'orphans and waifs in our institutional
structure'. He also said that Canada is 'playing with social operating agencies and
is not very clear why it is doing it . . . the real Canadian priority is to reform
government within the single public service and to adapt the public service into a
much more service orientated organisation'.[7]

Despite this point that the Canadian special operating agencies are only a
'demonstration project' and are not central to the current programme of reform,
there are some parallels with the issues faced by these agencies and those faced by
British Next Steps agencies. For example, the chief executive of the Canadian
Communications Group argued that he requires more freedoms, for example
with budgets, to enable him to run his organization effectively. However, the
Canadian special operating agencies experiment is so far limited in scope in that it
only extends to revenue raising operational units some of which are candidates
for privatization. By the end of May 1992 there had been no firm decisions on
whether the special operating agencies experiment should be extended to other
parts of government.

Departmental initiatives

The Public Service 2000 initiative and the creating of the special operating
agencies is a centrally led umbrella reform, run by the Public Service 2000
secretariat, which sets the framework and paves the way for departments to
devise and implement reforms within this major reform. The departmental reforms are about applying the framework of the Public Service 2000 initiative to
operational programmes and using the new delegations to their full effect to
improve service delivery.

One example of a departmental reform is the Health and Welfare Department's 'Income Security Programmes redesign business strategy'. This has involved a series of internal departmental reviews and consultations with the aim of
making sure that the department is organized in the best way to ensure 'excellence' in delivery of benefits:

> We must provide the right benefit, in the right amount, to the right client,
> at the right address, and on time. We must do this for every one of the 9
> million clients receiving benefit payments, every month of the year;[8]

'excellence' in delivery of client services,

> we aim to provide one call, one stop shopping (dealing with all of the
> client's income needs from one office), in a way which is accurate,
> efficient and respectful;[9]

'excellence' in accessibility to clients,

we must ensure that we have the resources, tools and planning to ensure that a client can reach us when he or she needs to.[10]

and 'excellence' in providing the management support that enables the department to achieve its targets for delivering benefits and services.

In summary then despite the similarities in the aims of the Canadian reforms there are some important differences in the approaches and substance of the British and Canadian reforms. The Canadian approach has the advantage that the extensive consultation procedures which have characterized Public Service 2000 coupled with the fact that departmental staff are also involved in developing and implementing their own reforms means that the large numbers involved in the reform process have become the owners of the reforms and therefore have a vested interest in their success. The down-side is that all this consultation has transaction costs and is slow which can result in a loss of momentum.

Comparing the substance of the Canadian reforms and the British Next Steps initiative

The effect on the public service

As for the differences between the substance of Canada's Public Service 2000 changes as compared with those of Britain's Next Steps initiative, we have seen that the Canadian emphasis is more on creating a unified public service and is more about restricting appointments from 'outside' than encouraging greater movement. (The Canadian public service has always had a far greater ability to bring in people at all levels – some 20 per cent of executives currently are recruited from 'outside'.)

The move to contract government

Canada has not gone so far down the Next Steps route of 'management by contract' but, similar to in Britain, there have been moves to strengthen existing reporting and accountability frameworks. For example, departments had widely defined objectives and produced performance information which related more to what was measurable than to departmental objectives. Departments and the Treasury Board are now working to tighten departmental objectives and to develop more useful performance measures.

Regarding the move to management of contract, in many ways Canada has more experience than Britain. Prior to the Public Service 2000 reforms, the Canadian fiscal crisis and the uncoordinated attempts to reduce quickly the size and expenditure of the public service had resulted in some radical measures. One example of this related to the policy of 'person year control' where restrictions were introduced on the numbers of staff which departments could employ as public servants and if departments needed any additional staff to do anything new or simply in order to perform their statutory roles in implementing existing policies, extra hands had to be brought from outside the public sector on a contract basis even where it may have been better value for money to employ additional 'in-house' staff. From 1992 departments can lapse 'person year controls' if it is more cost effective to carry out work 'in-house'. How this will work in practice however is still uncertain. A senior Treasury Board official speculated that 'The political environment with the major aim of reducing the public service will keep the focus on the numbers of employees in the public service rather than on the number of dollars spent.'[11] Canada has therefore been going down the track of 'management of contract' but not, like in Britain, as a positive policy.

Dividing 'policy' and 'operational' issues

Although the Canadian reforms have not concentrated on structural changes (despite the special operating agencies that have been set up as an 'experiment'), the reforms have encountered difficulties in clearly specifying who is responsible for what. Canada has attempted to side step the potential conflict between 'policy' and 'operational' issues by restricting its structural reforms. This means that the status quo continues. The Canadian status quo is that the Treasury Board and its minister are accountable to Parliament for 'policy' issues (for producing and communicating 'good' policies and for identifying where a policy is not working) and departments are accountable to Parliament for implementing those policies. Similar to the arrangements in Britain between executive agencies and departments, there is a blurring of responsibilities about who is accountable for what.

Autonomy and accountability

In this dilemma, Canada has experienced similar difficulties to those of Britain – how to encourage departmental efforts whilst ensuring that they remain accountable to central departments (Treasury Board) and to Parliament. A senior manager from the Treasury Board said,

> There has been an unbelievable push from departments for increased flexibilities . . . Treasury Board were regarded as a fairly major impediment to improving management. Many of the controls they had related less to good management than to particular ministers' concerns. They really could not justify the lack of department's powers.[12]

Again the issues are familiar, the granting of the new 'flexibilities' brings with it concerns about how they are going to be balanced with new arrangements to ensure the continuing accountability of departments to central departments and to Parliament. John Edwards outlines that the approach favoured has been 'letting a 1000 flowers bloom and giving time for Public Service 2000 to develop strong roots'.[13] He states, 'We have resisted making demands for work plans and for regular progress reports. However, it is often tough for Type A personalities to be patient.'[14] However he also raises the question about who will be responsible if things go wrong: 'Accountability under PS 2000 has yet to be put to strong tests. What will happen when reasonable risks are taken and there is a failure? What happens if it becomes a public issue?'[15]

The New Zealand reforms

The New Zealand reforms also grew out of a fiscal crisis. In 1984 a Labour Government was elected to face high fiscal deficits. It embarked on a programme of reform aiming to balance the books, including the removal of price and wage controls and the deregulation of the finance and other service sectors of the economy. Attention then turned to the state sector. In 1986 the major commercial operations of the government were 'corporatized' and given the principal objective to operate as successful businesses. Beginning in 1988 were the reforms to improve the performance of the core state sector. The objectives of the reform programme are familiar – to reduce public expenditure, enhance the efficiency and effectiveness of the public sector, improve the quality of the goods and services provided by public agencies, and ensure that providers are responsive to the needs and interests of their consumers. The methods adopted by the New Zealand reformers will also have a familiar ring to Next Steps followers:

> The reforms focused upon generating improvement by clarifying objectives and allowing managers freedom to manage within a framework of accountability and performance assessment. Improvement was to be achieved by better definition of the Government's strategy, decision making based upon clearly specified performance, delegating authority to chief executives to manage resources and improved reporting and assessment of performance.[16]

The process of New Zealand reform

In total contrast to the British experience, the main drivers in the New Zealand reform programme were the Treasury who drew up the main policy proposals on which the programme of reform came to be based. Also unlike in Britain, these proposals were detailed and drew heavily on a range of public administration, management and micro economic branches of theory.

The main features characterizing the New Zealand reforms (and again distinguishing them from those of Britain) have been the legislative changes. The two legal changes of most interest for the purposes of this book are:

The State Sector Act of 1988: The purposes of the State Sector Act were twofold.
　　It established a framework for a new relationship between the heads of departments and their ministers. The concept of a 'permanent head' of each department was replaced by that of a chief executive on a limited

tenure contract responsible to the minister for the performance of the department. Contracts with incentives for meeting performance agreements were also introduced for other senior executives. It created a new industrial relations and employment regime, giving heads of departments the power to hire and fire staff, and (within certain limits) to fix salaries within their departments (these functions used to be the responsibility of the central State Service Commission).

The Public Finance Act of 1989: This act gave the legislative framework to the financial reforms of: introducing a client/contractor divide into government departments; delegating financial responsibilities to departments for their capital assets; developing specified 'outputs' and measures by which departments' success in achieving these 'outputs' can be measured; to make ministers, not departments responsible for specifying what they want from each department and what each department must deliver.

The key elements of the New Zealand reforms were summarized in a presentation by a New Zealand delegate to a five countries meeting in Canada in 1990 to discuss the progress of their respective reforms:

1 The clarification of the *purposes* of each department or agency, with each being held responsible to produce defined and measured outputs at prices set by government as purchaser.
2 The rigorous definition of the *responsibility* of each chief executive for performance and management, with allied rewards and sanctions followed by the spread of this same pattern to subordinate layers of management.
3 The abolition of virtually all the detailed *input controls* traditionally administered by the Treasury and the State Services Commission, with the chief executives being given the power to hire and fire and to spend their allocations in the way which they considered best achieved their specified output objectives.
4 The requirement from government as owners to achieve defined *rates of return*, manage cash flows, set up full commercial style accounting and management information systems, and meet rigorous reporting requirements.
5 The requirement to *lift performance* immediately because of cuts in net funding.[17]

Comparing the substance of the New Zealand and British reforms

The New Zealand reforms have been described as the 'most ambitious and far reaching of their kind in the world'.[18] They have also been described as a 'culture shock' for the New Zealand public service.[19] The principles are very similar to Next Steps but the New Zealand reforms are faster and more radical. The following section outlines the ways in which the New Zealand reforms have tackled the dilemmas inherent in these types of reforms.

The dilemma of how to separate 'policy' and 'operational' issues

In Britain the lack of a clear dividing line between 'policy' and 'operational' issues results in a blurring of responsibilities between chief executives, permanent secretaries and ministers. The radical New Zealand reforms have limited these potential difficulties through an extreme solution. The level of contracting is higher than in Britain. In New Zealand, ministers remain accountable to Parliament for all policy matters and they are also responsible for buying all the services required from that department. For example, in the case of social welfare the minister is responsible for buying services from three types of business units: output delivery business units – the Income Support Service, the Children and Young Persons Service, the Community Funding Agency, the Social Policy Agency and Ministerial Services; support services business units – Information Technology, Legal Services and Corporate Services; corporate management business units – Finance, Resource Management, Audit and Security, Cultural Liaison. Each of these units has a business plan and the output delivery units have a budget and specified targets of the outputs they must achieve with that money. The support units must sell their services to the output delivery units, who are increasingly free to purchase such services from outside the department. The heads of each of the business units are accountable to Parliament for the day to day running of their unit – in the case of the Ministerial Services unit and the Social Policy Agency, this may involve providing complete, reliable and timely policy advice. The minister is responsible for ensuring that these business units are doing what they are supposed to be doing and that he or she is achieving value for money in his or her purchases. The minister is also responsible for any policy decisions. Such a structure avoids the obfuscation as to the appropriate role of departmental headquarters and permanent secretaries.

Accountability versus autonomy

The autonomy versus accountability tension has also been evident in New Zealand but rather than resulting in restrictions on freedoms it has resulted in attempts to specify personal accountability clearly and in a concentrated effort on developing 'output' performance information. As we have seen above, the fact that the level of contracting is higher means that it is easier to define clearly who is responsible for what.

One difficulty with the new arrangements of ministers 'buying' services from their departments is that their workload has increased and that there is little in the way of a 'centre' to support ministers in their role of ensuring that departments are doing what they are supposed to be doing. In some ways, the New Zealand reforms are now backtracking because of a recognition of this gap and the numbers of staff involved in providing this 'central support' is now increasing.

The effect on the public service

The effect of the New Zealand reforms on its public service has been radical. The service has declined from some 85,000 staff in 1988 to some 33,000 staff in 1992. As we have seen, similarly to Britain, there has also been an increase in the use of 'contracts' and an undermining of the principle of the public service as a secure job for life. There have also been concerns that the changes have been undermining the professionalism of the public service and that, for example, the quality of its draft legislation is not as good as it was which means that Members are now having to spend more time in committee considering the legislation.

Conclusions

Returning to our original questions, the comparisons between the British, New Zealand and Canadian reforms show us that there are many similarities in the factors prompting the reforms, notably, in the financial difficulties facing each of these countries at the time when the reforms were launched. What is interesting is that each of the countries responded to similar conditions by adopting different strategies. Britain and New Zealand went down the line of structural change whereas Canada followed the model of reforming existing structures. These differences in approaches can in part be explained by what went before. Certainly in Britain, there had already been a series of attempts at reform within existing arrangements (with varying degrees of success). By contrast, Canada had already tried the course of structural reform and now wanted to move towards the existing British model of a unified professional public service. Whatever the approach or the reasons for a particular model being adopted, an important insight which the comparisons have allowed us to make is that none of the solutions adopted by any of the countries have been fully successful in overcoming the central difficulties of how to distinguish between policy and operational issues or how to balance autonomy and accountability.

Notes

1 The Government of Canada (1990) *Public Service 2000: The Renewal of the Public Service of Canada*. Ottawa, Ministry of Supply and Services, December; Treasury Board of Canada (1990) *PS2000: Summaries of the Reports of the Task Forces*. Ottawa, Ministry of Supply and Services.
2 Privy Council Office (1990) PS2000 Briefing Note, *PS2000 – What's it all about?*. Ottawa, Ministry of Supply and Services. September; emphasis in original document.
3 Office of the Prime Minister (1989) *Public Service 2000*. Ottawa, Ministry of Supply and Services. 12 December.

4 Interview with John Edwards, 4 May 1992.
5 The Government of Canada (1990) op. cit.
6 The Government of Canada (1990) op. cit.
7 Interview with John Edwards, 4 May 1992.
8 Health and Welfare Canada (1990) *Income Security Programs Vision*. Ottawa, Ministry of Supply and Services.
9 Ibid.
10 Ibid.
11 Interview with senior Treasury Board official, 5 May 1992.
12 Ibid.
13 J. Edwards (1991) Notes for a Presentation to Senior Management of Consumer and Corporate Affairs, Alymer. Unpublished document, September.
14 Ibid.
15 Ibid.
16 Para. 2, State Services Commission (1991) *Steering Group Review of State Sector Reforms*. Wellington, Ministry of Supply and Services.
17 New Zealand Paper presented to the Five Countries meeting, Canada (1990) *Special Executive Agencies and the Delivery of Social Security Benefits*. Unpublished document.
18 State Services Commission (1991) op. cit.
19 New Zealand Paper presented to the Five Countries meeting, Canada (1990) op. cit.

9

Evaluating Next Steps

There are many criteria by which Next Steps can be assessed. The first is whether it is achieving its specified objectives of 'creating durable improvements in management in government and delivering services more efficiently and effectively within available resources for the benefit of customers, tax payers and staff'. In other words, there are three main criteria by which the success of Next Steps in meeting its formal objectives can be judged: Is Next Steps resulting in a more efficient and effective civil service? Are 'customers' happy with the service they are receiving? Are staff happy with the new arrangements?

The formal Next Steps objectives are not however the only criteria by which it can be evaluated. Next Steps can also be judged in terms of what it tells us about administrative theory and in terms of its durability and longer term consequences. This chapter therefore also analyses what Next Steps tells us about administrative theory and considers the future development of Next Steps and its wider implications.

The 'success' of Next Steps in achieving its formal objectives

Of course the real world is not a perfect research laboratory and there is no perfect way of evaluating Next Steps in achieving its stated objectives of improving efficiency, effectiveness and quality of service. The ideal way of judging 'success' using these criteria would be by using consistent measures of efficiency, effectiveness and customer and staff attitudes which stemmed from before Next Steps and continued into the future. In the ideal laboratory all other factors which may affect the chosen measures should also be held constant so that we could be sure that any changes in efficiency and effectiveness or in attitudes were a direct result of Next Steps. Since we are lacking the ideal data and the ideal research conditions this chapter examines what data central departments and agencies have been using to evaluate changes in efficiency and effectiveness and changes in 'customer' and staff attitudes and considers what this data tells us about the success of Next Steps.

Improvements in efficiency and effectiveness

Next Steps resulted in some major changes to departments' and agencies' reporting and information systems including some important changes to their selection of performance measures and targets. Chapter 5 has outlined how agency performance indicators and high level targets were selected and revised (by central departments and agencies) to reflect agencies' newly reviewed agency objectives and 'business' aims. Most agencies' performance measures therefore either measure different things or measure the same things on a different basis than earlier departmental measures of the efficiency and effectiveness of agency operations. So, we cannot yet simply look at changes in agencies' high level measures of efficiency and effectiveness to assess whether Next Steps has directly resulted in some improvements.

What we can do is look at how successful agencies are being in meeting their new key performance targets. In some instances it was difficult to set these targets where there was little existing information on performance in particular areas. However, most of the targets are based on existing information about how efficiently and effectively departmental operations performed particular functions in the pre-Next Steps days. Many of the targets are also fairly tight as they assume that agencies will achieve efficiency savings over and above the 1.5 per cent expected from all departments.

The Office of Public Service and Science have pulled together the success of the agencies established to date in meeting their targets in the 1991/92 year. Table 9.1 summarizes the results of all the agencies. It shows that overall agencies met about three out of four of their targets. The area where

Table 9.1 The percentage of key performance targets achieved by executive agencies in 1991–92

Quality targets %	Financial targets %	Efficiency targets %	Throughput targets %
79	73	76	76

Source: adapted from Office of Public Service and Science (1992) *The Next Steps Agencies Review 1992*, Cm 2111. London, HMSO.

Table 9.2   The percentage of key performance targets met by all agencies in 1991–92 year compared with the percentage of key performance targets met by the social security agencies

	Quality targets %	Financial targets %	Efficiency targets %	Throughput targets %
All agencies	79	73	76	76
DSS agencies	93	83	100	90

Source: adapted from Office of Public Service and Science (1992) *The Next Steps Agencies Review 1992,* Cm 211. London, HMSO.

performance was least good overall however was in meeting the financial targets. Richard Mottram, the current Next Steps project manager, is clearly pleased with the overall results. He refers to them saying,

> in general, the results are good. Around three out of four targets have been met, a similar picture to last year. For those Agencies which have existed for more than a year, the key targets will have become more demanding over time and the figures indicate continuing improvement in performance.[1]

Table 9.2 compares the overall performance of agencies in general in meeting their targets with that of the four Department of Social Security agencies which were up and running at that time – the Benefits Agency, the Contributions Agency, the Information Technology Services Agency and the Resettlement Agency. It shows that the performance of the Department of Social Security's agencies, as judged by these criteria, was above that of the average of the other agencies. The following section considers some examples in more detail of what the performance of the Department of Social Security's agencies in achieving the key performance indicators tells us about the success of Next Steps.

The Benefits Agency

Table 9.3, taken from the Department of Social Security's annual report for 1993 shows, in more detail, the key performance results of the benefits agency. The results look impressive with only three targets not being met – the efficiency savings, family credit accuracy and the percentage of lone parents receiving maintenance. On close inspection, a fourth target was also not met – the financial target of living within budget. The original budgetary allocation and target was for £1,707.5 million but this was supplemented during the year because of increased workloads and increased to the shown £1,772.6 million. The effect of external factors on the success of agencies in meeting their targets was highlighted in Chapter 5 but it is important to raise again in evaluating the success of

Table 9.3   Benefits Agency: Key performance targets and results 1991–92

Service delivery	Target 91–92	Result 91–92
Social Fund, community care grant clearance	7 days	5.9 days
Social Fund, crisis loans clearance	same day	same day
Social Fund, proportion of gross loan expenditure to be covered by loan recoveries	£143m[a]	£147.5m
Social Fund, live within gross allocation for loans and grants	£277.4m	£276m
Income Support, claims clearance	5 days	4 days
Income Support, accuracy[b]	93%	95.7%
Sickness and Invalidity Benefit claims clearance	9 days	7 days
Incapacity benefits, accuracy	96.5%	96.5%
Family Credit, claims clearance	60% in 18 days[c] 85% in 35 days	64.4% 89.2%
Family Credit, fastpath claims	90% in 5 days	92.1%
Family Credit, accuracy	93%	91.5%
War Pensions, disablement claims clearance	75% in 195 days	71.3%
War Pensions, widowhood claims	80% in 90 days	80.9%
Liable relatives, annual benefit savings	£300m	£283.9m
Liable relatives, % of lone parents on IS receiving maintenance	27%	21%
Fraud, gross annual benefit savings	£382m	£416m
Overpayment recovery, gross cash	£18m	£24.2m
Efficiency, achieve cumulative running costs efficiency savings reflected in net budget figure of	£188.3m	£196.2m
Finance, living within budget	£1,772.6m[d]	£1,769.6m
Customer satisfaction, proportion of customers expressing satisfaction with the service they have received (%)	85%	86%

(a) This target was originally set as a % recovery figure but was amended during the year.
(b) The target outturns reported here are based on line management returns. They are tested by internal audit and the National Audit Office (NAO) and recent evidence indicates there are some differences between the results of management and audit. These differences are being pursued.
(c) The target definition was changed from a calculated average to a formula based clearance time.
(d) The figure of £1,707.5 million quoted in the business plan was the amount initially allocated by ministers. The final allocation of £1,772.5 million takes account of internal transfer during the year and additional resources allocated to the Agency because of increased workloads.

Source: Department of Social Security Annual Report, Cm 2213 (1993) London, HMSO.

agencies. The Department of Social Security's annual report argued that the Benefits Agency targets missed were 'particularly affected by external factors such as higher than anticipated workloads and unexpectedly high unemployment'.[2]

In an attempt to overcome this difficulty the department is now looking at new ways of workload forecasting and finding a more flexible way of matching available resources to workloads. The Department of Social Security do however accept that problems with workload forecasting were not the only reasons for some of the Benefits Agency targets not being met.

The Contributions Agency and the Resettlement Agency

The Contributions Agency and the Resettlement Agency were the most successful of the Department of Social Security's agencies in terms of meeting their 'key performance targets' in 1991–92. As we saw in Chapter 5, there were some particular problems in devising performance measures and targets for the Resettlement Agency as the work had always been given a relatively low priority and consequently little information was available, for example, on the effectiveness of the agency in terms of 'resettling' its clients. Some of the key Resettlement Agencies' performance measures were therefore 'throughput' measures, for example, of devising measuring standards by a particular date rather than of actually measuring the effectiveness of the units in resettling their residents. The fact that the agency achieved all its targets therefore tells us nothing about the success of Next Steps in improving the effectiveness of the agency or the quality of service provided by the units. The measures do however tell us that the Resettlement Agency has been a Next Steps success in terms of being more efficient by living within budget and by achieving efficiency savings over its target.

Table 9.4, again taken from the Department of Social Security's annual report, shows that the Contributions Agency met and in most cases, exceeded its targets in 1991–92. What these results actually tell us about the success of Next Steps is however limited. They do tell us that the agency has stayed within budget and has achieved efficiency savings but beyond that all the results tell us is that the agency has successfully been rectifying previous shortcomings by identifying and collecting outstanding arrears. The choice of indicators and targets for the Contributions Agency will have to change because the 'pot' of outstanding arrears reduces when the agency is successful in collecting the outstanding contributions. The Contributions Agency results tell us nothing about the effectiveness of the agency in keeping accurate national insurance contribution records or in providing a good quality of service to customers. These shortcomings are, at least in part, now being rectified as the agency has introduced two new targets for 1992–93 – the level of customer satisfaction and the 'clearance of rejected items' (rejected items refer to national insurance contributions paid for that the agency cannot identify the records on which they should be recorded).

Table 9.4 Contributions Agency targets and results 1991–92

	Target	Performance
Financial		
Complete work programme within budget	£121.45m	£121.37m
Achieve cumulative efficiency savings	£3.40m	£3.77m
Compliance		
Increase collection of arrears (excluding central payments section) by 10% of 1990–91 outturn	£218m	£218.3m
Increase class 1 arrears identified from survey by 35%	£17.5m	£38.9m
Increase identified in-year class 1 adjustment by 35%	£16.3m	£20.33m
Increase the number of new class 2 contributors identified	60,000	84,040
Increase the number of surveys by 10%	88,000	106,353
Records maintenance		
Post x% of available end of year returns by 31 December	98%	99.15%
Clear x% of benefit enquiries handled . . .	99%	99.71%
clerically in 3 working days of y% accuracy	98%	99.23%
Customer service/information provision		
Register x% of acceptable personal pension applications in 28 working days	90%	100%
Answer x% of employer, contributor and personal pension enquiries within 10 working days	95%	97.75%

Source: Department of Social Security Annual Report, Cm 2213 (1993) London, HMSO.

These examples of Department of Social Security agencies which appear to demonstrate that Next Steps has been a great success in terms of achieving its formal objectives therefore show that these overall results should be treated with caution. Although the results tell us that the agencies have been largely successful in meeting their specified targets it does not necessarily follow that Next Steps has been achieving its formal objectives of improving efficiency, effectiveness and quality of service. What the targets are measuring and how they are set is still developing and also, factors other than the introduction of Next Steps may affect an agency's performance. First, it is possible that Next Steps may experience a 'Hawthorne honeymoon' where performance improves as a direct consequence of the fact that it is a time of change but the improvements are not a result of what the changes actually are and will fade over time. Second, we have already seen how the problem of unemployment rising affected the success of the Benefits Agency in achieving its financial targets. Other external factors which may affect an agency's performance, either positively or adversely, include other organizational changes (such as the full implementation of the social security

computerization – the operational strategy) or policy changes such as the introduction of the new disability benefits.

So, at present it would be misleading to assess whether Next Steps is
working in terms of achieving its formal objectives of improving effectiveness
and efficiency by evaluating it in terms of agencies' success in meeting their key
performance targets. Other considerations also must be taken into account
including the fact that targets are still developing and that other, external
factors, may also affect an agency's performance. In addition, there is always the
possibility that targets are being set low so as to make Next Steps a public
relations success both within and outside Whitehall. The key performance
targets are however the only available overall measures of the success of Next
Steps in meeting its formal objectives and they appear to suggest that, on the
whole, agencies have been achieving their targets.

Improvement in quality of service

One of the central planks of Next Steps which has been given added weight by
the Citizen's Charter is the aim of improving quality of service to the 'customer'. Customer opinion surveys are by no means new to the civil service and
they are certainly not new to the Department of Social Security. The Department of Social Security introduced reviews of 'customers'' experiences of
claiming social security benefits in 1984 and these reviews were revamped in
1987 and 1988. The introduction of Next Steps has however witnessed many
more changes to the ways in which the Department of Social Security and its
agencies have been reviewing customer satisfaction. The department's agencies
have all taken the responsibility for their own customer opinion surveys.

The Benefits Agency's customer opinion survey was introduced in 1991.
The sample is drawn nationally from 159 districts. The main change from the
old quality assessment package is that it is a centrally conducted survey and it is
not now possible to disaggregate the data to see how the performance of each
district or local office compares. This gap is however partly being filled by local
surveys with districts conducting their own surveys.

The main point about the introduction of the new surveys is that the
method of assessment has changed which means that it is not possible to
evaluate how customer opinions have changed since the introduction of Next
Steps. There has even been a change in the Benefits Agency's 1992 customer
opinion survey as compared with its 1991 survey. There have been changes to
the ways in which the samples are weighted in an attempt to capture people
who move on and off income support. The rationale behind the change was to
make the survey more robust but one adverse effect of the change is that the
results of the 1992 survey will not be directly comparable with the results of the
1991 survey.

In summary then, within the Department of Social Security, it is not
possible to carry out a 'before' and 'after' evaluation of how Next Steps has
affected 'customers'' perceptions of the services they receive. The Department

of Social Security agencies have been concentrating on developing and improving their customer opinion surveys which, if these are continued on the same basis, will lead to some comparability of opinions over time but, as yet, this is not possible.

Staff attitudes

Again, there are no before and after surveys to evaluate how Next Steps has affected staff attitudes within the Department of Social Security's agencies. However, against the background of the development of Next Steps and other changes within the organization of operations of the department, for example, resulting from the computerization of social security benefits, the Department of Social Security did commission the Institute for Manpower Studies (IMS) to find out:

- how well staff coped with the change;
- how they feel about the way they are managed, the work they do and their prospects;
- how motivated they are in their jobs;
- how they view their future.[3]

Some 120 staff took part in semi-structured detailed interviews and group discussions prior to the questionnaire design so as to ensure that the questionnaire addressed issues of concern to them. The department's agencies and headquarters were also consulted to ensure that they were happy with the questionnaires and that questions specific to each were included. After testing the questionnaire with some initial interviews it was sent to 12,000 staff in the Department of Social Security's agencies and headquarters. It is not possible from the survey's results to assess whether or not staff are 'happier' under the new post-Next Steps regime than they were before but there are some interesting findings. To quote directly from the digest of the research findings which was circulated to Department of Social Security staff:

> Staff were asked a number of questions aimed at establishing how they felt about a number of features of working in the Department. They rated a number as being of particular importance to them . . . When the extent to which staff said they had actually *experienced* these features positively are examined, some important discrepancies emerge. In particular, 'good pay', 'having job satisfaction' and 'promotion based on merit' are felt to be important by staff, yet do not register very high levels of 'experience'.
>
> On several other aspects of work, staff are moderately satisfied. 'Good job security' was a source of satisfaction, along with 'having an approachable boss', 'working in a friendly atmosphere' and 'flexible working hours'. There was less satisfaction with 'working for a well-managed organisation', the number of 'promotion opportunities' and 'opportunities to train and develop'.[4]

What is interesting is that some of the key elements of Next Steps do not rate well on the survey. 'Having job satisfaction' was rated as important by staff but was not always experienced. The aim of the Next Steps delegation of responsibility was to free those on the coal face to get on with their work which should, at least in theory, increase their job satisfaction. Another factor of concern raised by the survey was that staff did not appear to be satisfied with the management of their organization. These feelings could be influenced by the fact that staff have been experiencing a lot of change and that once the dust has settled they may feel happier with their management regime. A further finding from the staff attitudes survey of particular interest was that staff 'were not motivated to work harder by performance pay'. As we have seen, the Next Steps thrust towards group bonuses and individual performance pay is predicated on the belief that pay is a compelling factor in motivation. This Department of Social Security staff attitude survey may suggest that this conjecture is ill founded.

In summary, the Department of Social Security's staff attitude does not tell us anything about the effect of Next Steps on staff attitudes as again, we have no 'before' and 'after' picture of how attitudes have changed. As Next Steps is still in its incubation period, the survey comes too early to tell us about how staff will feel in a post-Next Steps regime once the dust has settled. The existing survey does however highlight some concerns which need to be considered and addressed.

Contribution of administrative theory to Next Steps and of Next Steps to administrative theory

Next Steps raises a number of issues relating to administrative theories which have been explored throughout the text. Chapters 1 and 2 asked whether the ideas behind Next Steps are new and where they have come from. They concluded that the ideas are not new but are rooted in theory and in practice. The ideas are a part of a line of reforms which have come to be commonly known as the 'new public management'. In turn, this line of reforms is rooted in public choice theory and agency theory. In addition, other more traditional branches of administrative theory informed other themes which have been explored throughout the text – the difficulties in distinguishing 'policy' and 'operational' issues; the apparent dichotomy between accountability and flexibility; and the move to contract government. This section draws together the theoretical themes which have been raised throughout the book and evaluates their contribution to Next Steps and, in turn, the contribution of the Next Steps experience to administrative theory and its application to other areas of public policy.

The client/contractor divide

One of the key features of Next Steps is the development of contracts to manage operational activities to be carried out either by the public sector or increasingly, particularly as the Market Testing initiative matures, by the private sector. Next Steps is about the move to management by contract and has now, with the introduction of the Market Testing initiative, also come to be about the move to management of contract. There are parallels with these developments and the current move to develop quasi-markets which is common to many areas of public sector service delivery including health, personal social services, education, housing and a number of local government services such as refuse collection. Next Steps application of the client/contractor divide throughout the entire existing civil service and right to the core of government is a major test of the structures and principles of introducing quasi-markets into public services. So, what does Next Steps tell us about the client/contractor divide and its application to other areas of public policy?

The first finding is that the introduction of a client/contractor divide into areas of public policy transforms the character of the administrative body. In the civil service the main implications of this move to management by contract and of the move to management of contract have been for the existing organization, culture and for the skills required by civil servants.

In the civil service there have been two phases of change. Phase one has been the introduction of management by contract with the Next Steps structural change of creating agencies and of managing these agencies through a series of 'contracts' (the framework documents, business plans and corporate plans). A part of this move to management by contract has also been the arrangements between agencies (through 'service level agreements') where one party 'contracts' another to provide certain goods or services within a specified level of resources. Civil servants are now either 'clients' or 'contractors' and some may be both. For example, an agency may be contracted to its minister but it may also be the 'client' of another agencies' services – for example, the Social Security Contributions Agency is 'contracted' to collect national insurance contributions, to keep the national insurance contribution records and to provide the information to other agencies but it is also the 'client' of the computer services provided by another of the department's agencies, the Information Technology Services Agency.

The introduction of these new arrangements has required agencies to establish distinct organizational structures and for headquarters also to review their roles and organization. It has resulted in agencies being provided with greater freedoms to become more effective 'contractors' in meeting with the demands of their business plans. These 'flexibilities' have in turn, undermined the existing uniformity in civil service organization within departments and in pay and grading arrangements. The introduction of the client/contractor divide has also required civil servants to learn new skills. It has resulted in pressures for central departments (the Office of the Minister for the Civil Service, the Treasury and departmental headquarters) to become professional 'clients' in terms of learning how to draw up 'contracts' and to manage these 'contracts' which, in turn, have resulted in greater demands for better performance information. Until recently the tendering, controlling of and writing of contracts was the undisputed territory of the private sector.

The second phase of change in the civil service has been the move to management of contract which has largely been precipitated by the recent Market Testing initiative. The Market Testing initiative means that civil service 'contractors' are increasingly having to compete with the private sector in securing the contract to provide certain goods or services. This second phase blurs the boundaries between the public and private sectors and this 'blurring' has some important implications for the future of the civil service and for other areas of public policy which adopt similar strategies.

One implication is that it may undermine public service loyalty. We have all met people who work for wages lower than they could command in the private sector because of their belief in the 'public sector'. The introduction of private sector values into the public service through the client/contractor divide could undermine this public service loyalty and, in some cases, their willingness to work for less money (particularly if civil servants are regularly having to compete with others from outside for their jobs). A further consequence which will be particularly important especially once the Market Testing initiative is in full swing and is also being applied to core functions such as the paying of social security benefits and the collection of national insurance contributions, is that it will reduce the ability of administrators to respond to environmental or policy developments. Equally, 'clients' can no longer incrementally change their requirements to match changing assumptions or priorities. Finally, the most important consequence of contracting-out services or functions is that the change would be long term and would most likely be irreversible. Once services are contracted-out of the public service, the public service providers are no longer around to compete for subsequent tenders. Contracting-out will result in a loss of expertise within the public sector.

Transaction costs

The second finding which Next Steps tells us about the application of the client/contractor divide to other areas of public policy is that it involves additional transaction costs. As Chapter 2 demonstrated, the branch of agency theory, transaction cost analysis, illuminates the additional costs involved in establishing and retaining semi-autonomous executive agencies. Transaction cost analysis was originally developed to explain the growth of large firms in capitalist societies. Essentially the theory is that there are costs involved in a principal controlling an agent and that firms expand to minimize these costs. Firms either integrate vertically, that is, with those from whom they are purchasing a service or goods, or horizontally, that is, with any competitors. Transaction cost analysis contrasts with the Next Steps theory that the increased flexibility and autonomy ensuing from devolvement will result in greater efficiency and effectiveness. So, do the theories of transaction costs analysis only apply to private sector industries and is the public sector different?

Chapter 1 has already demonstrated that transaction cost theories are a useful model in identifying the additional costs of establishing executive agencies. There are clearly three types of transaction costs in any agency arrangement: the transitional costs, the periodic costs and the permanent costs.

Transitional costs

The transitional costs of establishing Next Steps have been high. It would be extremely difficult however to even estimate what these costs have been as much of the information is not available and even that information which could be available has not been collected either on a departmental or central department (the Treasury or the Office of Public Service and Science) basis.

The transitional costs of implementing Next Steps and establishing agencies include the costs of establishing the necessary structures, the information systems and the reporting arrangements. These may include the costs of relocating staff or of moving staff to other agencies and of recruiting new staff. Such costs were incurred as a result of the Social Security Contributions Agency centralizing staff who were previously dispersed throughout the local office network. Other Next Steps transitional costs include the costs of agencies developing 'training strategies', 'personnel strategies' and 'corporate identities' (through marketing techniques such as developing agency newsletters or issuing agency scarves and agency mugs to staff). They may also include increasing the pay budget within an agency now in the expectation of efficiency savings over a specified period of say five to 10 years. On a more down to earth note, there were also costs involved in organizing social occasions to mark the launch of the agencies.

The information on transitional costs which is not available are those costs which are not easily distinguishable from the day to day work of a department or agency such as the costs of staff meetings to discuss changes. Amongst the costs which could be distinguished are those of civil servants acquiring new skills. This has involved the extensive use of management consultants who have been involved in advising agencies and departments on how to develop the appropriate structures, systems and reporting arrangements. Developing Next Steps has meant big business for management consultants and yet information on the overall costs of all this is not publicly available.

Periodic costs

The periodic costs of establishing Next Steps include the costs of reviewing staff's and agencies' 'contracts'. For example 'periodic costs' include the costs of possibly advertising externally and interviewing potential chief executives every three to five years as a means of ensuring that the agency has the best person for the job – even if, after this process, the person in post is reappointed. In addition, the agency framework documents which establish the operational structures within which agencies may operate, at present, must be 'revised' about every three years. 'Revising' these documents will involve a series of meetings between central departments and agencies and therefore 'costs'. The agency business plans have to be revised every year and the agency reports also have to be written every year.

Once the Market Testing initiative has taken root and more services are contracted-out, the costs of tendering and contracting for departmental or agencies' services will also involve costs. The Williamson analysis outlined in Chapter 1 has also shown that these 'periodic' transaction costs are likely to be higher in dealings with specialist agencies or service providers. This is because these agencies and service providers and their staff are in a strong bargaining position in negotiating their contracts, particularly when there are few others competing for their work.

Permanent costs

The permanent costs of the Next Steps arrangements are a direct consequence of reverting to the 1960s belief in small being beautiful. What is lost are the economies of scale for example, of running one personnel section and one finance section for a large department such as the Department of Social Security.

The Williamson analysis of transaction costs therefore shows some of the costs involved in developing Next Steps. Although it is not, at present, possible to put a figure on these costs, it is clear they are high. This means that Next Steps has a big job to do in ensuring that these costs continue to be offset, for example, through efficiency savings.

The policy versus operations dichotomy

The application of the client/contractor divide to the civil service also informs us that administrative theory was right to insist that 'policy' and 'operations' cannot be separated. As we have seen, Next Steps attempts to separate responsibilities for 'policy' and 'operational' functions and to define clearly the responsibilities of each party in the framework documents. The Next Steps experience has shown that there is a direct relationship between the 'type' of agency and degree of difficulty caused by the obfuscation between 'policy' and 'operational' issues. Again referring back to our typology of agencies outlined in Table 1.3, it is those agencies in box 3 in particular (the monopoly Treasury dependent agencies) which have caused and are likely to continue to cause the greatest difficulties in this respect (agencies in this category include the Department of Social Security's Benefits Agency, War Pensions Agency, Contributions Agency and Child Support Agency). The type of work in which these agencies are involved is closer to the core of government and consequently more politically sensitive. The questions raised are therefore whether the Next Steps (public choice theory) principles of separating functions can be equally applied across all areas of government or whether they can only be fully applied where the degree of political involvement has traditionally been lower, such as has been the case for the Department of Social Security's Information Technology Services Agency.

The tension between accountability and flexibility

The conclusion that the Next Steps principles must be applied to varying degrees depending on the 'type' of agency is also supported by Next Steps' experiences of balancing accountability and flexibility. Chapter 1 has shown that public administration literature has comprehensively addressed the conflict between flexibility and parliamentary accountability,[5] and yet inherent in Next Steps are the aims of increasing both flexibility and accountability.

The early evidence coming from the Prime Minister's Efficiency Unit was that rather than flexibility and accountability balancing, accountability was triumphing over flexibility.[6] There is also some evidence that the Treasury has been more ruled by its traditional concerns of controlling public expenditure than by its wish to see agencies developing into semi-autonomous bodies (see Chapter 4). The block to change raised by the Treasury, at least initial reluctance, to play the Next Steps game was added to by some legal difficulties over delegating agencies additional 'flexibilities' until the Civil Service Management Functions act was passed in 1993. Now that this act has been passed and there appears to be a change in the air with the Treasury's officials now apparently actively encouraging agencies to seek additional flexibilities (see Chapter 4), Next Steps looks set to run – at least, in some areas.

Again an important difference is emerging in how Next Steps is being applied to different areas of government and different 'types' of agencies. The Department of Social Security remains fairly reticent about loosening the reins on the politically sensitive Benefits Agency. The accountability versus flexibility dichotomy is therefore creating more tensions in areas closer to the core of government which have a higher political profile than in other, less contentious, areas of government.

Next Steps lessons

The main lesson emerging from Next Steps is that its unintended consequences are likely to be more important than the aims set out in any Next Steps policy documents or discussed in any formal Next Steps debates.

The main unintended consequence is for the constitutional role of the civil service. The political neutrality of civil servants could be threatened by the increasing use of short term contracts to appoint people outside the civil service directly to senior positions, particularly if these direct appointments are also extended to apply to headquarters posts. The longer term implication of this is that each change in government could see a change in the outlooks of those holding senior civil servants' posts, as and when their contracts come up for renewal.

Next Steps may also reduce the anaesthetizing effect of the civil service on radical reform. First, Next Steps may change the nature of the relationship between civil servants and ministers as those civil servants on short term appointments may be more committed to the task of pleasing their ministers than to servicing the civil service traditions. Second, the infiltration of the civil service by different 'types' of people, with experience of business, finance and industry, is likely to change the character of the civil service making it more pro-active and less resistant to change.

A second effect of Next Steps is to raise the question of what is a 'department' and how 'departments' and 'agencies' should be represented in the Cabinet. As agencies increasingly develop as semi-autonomous bodies the rationale for what holds a set of agencies together under the umbrella of one department comes increasingly into question. When asked about what holds a 'department' together one senior official said that it was the public expenditure round. If this is the case then this rationale will increasingly reduce as agencies are increasingly responsible for carrying out their own bidding in the public expenditure round and in some cases are increasingly expanding in new markets which may not directly relate to the work of their 'department'.

A third apparently unintended but nevertheless important consequence of Next Steps is that it is changing existing traditions of parliamentary accountability. Next Steps both directly and indirectly affects the fundamental principles of parliamentary accountability. The main threat is being posed by the Market Testing initiative which involves contracting-out existing government functions. At present the Market Testing initiative is concentrating on service functions but as it develops to include tendering core government functions such as the paying of social security benefits, Parliament must ensure that it continues to have some rights of access to look at how those services are being delivered.

In summary then, this book has demonstrated that Next Steps is an evolutionary revolution. It is evolutionary in two ways. First, many of its ideas and features are not new. Second, it has evolved from the time of the Efficiency Unit report which launched the initiative. Unlike in New Zealand, Next Steps had no blueprint of where it was going or what it was to achieve by when. It was launched with some radical ideas about creating semi-autonomous executive agencies but many of the other features of the current stages of reform were not made explicit at the time of the Efficiency Unit report. The changes set in place by Next Steps have gathered increasing momentum and change is now moving fast, particularly now the Market Testing initiative has completed its first phase.

This chapter has asked whether all this change is achieving Next Steps specified formal objective of improving efficiency and quality of service for the benefit of customers, tax payers and staff. One success of Next Steps is quite clear, namely its success in achieving change. By 5 April 1993, 89 agencies had been established and over 260,000 civil servants (45 per cent of all civil servants) are working in agencies. The creation of agencies has required departments to look at their overall role and many functions and ask why they are doing certain things and whether they are doing them in the most efficient way. Such questions cannot be bad.

Shortcomings in the data available to date make it impossible to confidently say whether or not Next Steps has increased efficiency and quality of service and whether staff are now happier. The information that is available on efficiency and quality of service does, however, look promising. Most agencies have achieved the majority of their targets (although this begs the question of whether the targets have been stringent enough or whether they were set with the aim in mind of making Next Steps look a success). Equally the Department of Social Security's staff attitudes survey which was conducted in 1992 is by no means a tale of gloom and despair.

The changes to date are foundations for the major challenges to come. The Market Testing initiative will increasingly result in the contracting-out of existing civil service functions to private sector contractors and will be critical to the future shape and role of the civil service.

Notes

1 R. Mottram in Foreword to OPSS (1992) *The Next Steps Agencies Review 1992*, Cm 2111. London, HMSO.
2 Para. 195, Department of Social Security (1993) *The Government's Expenditure Plans 1993–94 to 1995–96*, Cm 2213. London, HMSO.
3 Institute for Manpower Studies (1993) *Survey Results Digest: Staff Attitudes in the Department of Social Security*. London, Institute for Manpower Studies, March.
4 Ibid.
5 For example, P. Self (1972) *Administrative Theories and Politics*. London, George Allen and Unwin.
6 Efficiency Unit (1991) *Making the Most of Next Steps: The Management of Ministers' Departments and Their Executive Agencies*. London, HMSO.

Index

140   Transforming central government

recruitment, 65–6, 100–2
and transitional costs, 129
see also civil servants
surveys, of customer satisfaction, 124–5

targets of agencies, 68–75
success in achieving, 119–24, 133
Thatcher, Margaret, 27
throughput targets of agencies, 119, 120, 122
trade unions, 46, 53–4, 60
Training and Enterprise Councils (TECs), 85
transaction costs, 17–20, 26, 78, 128–30
transitional transaction costs, 17, 18
of establishing Next Steps, 129
Treasury
and agencies' financial and personnel flexibilities, 50–1, 63–4
and agencies' pay and grading, 98, 99
and agency chief executives, 61
and agency framework documents, 61, 63–4
and client/contractor relationships, 127
and the development of monitoring arrangements, 49–50

forecasting agencies' workload, 79
and the National Audit Office, 56
and Next Steps, 48–51
and the Office of Public Service and Science (OPSS), 46
and transitional costs, 129
Treasury and Civil Service Select Committee, 23, 55, 65
and parliamentary accountability, 82, 89, 91, 93
Treasury dependent monopoly agencies, 39–41, 130
Tullock, G., 15

unemployment, and Benefits Agency targets, 123

Vehicle Inspectorate, 20, 57, 86, 87, 97

Waldegrave, William, 23, 48
War Pensions Agency, 32, 35, 36, 37
as Treasury dependent monopoly agency, 40–1, 130
Weber, Max, 15
Whitehall actors, 45, 46, 47–54
Williamson, Oliver, 17, 18, 19, 20

PRIVATIZATION AND REGULATORY CHANGE IN EUROPE

Michael Moran and Tony Prosser (eds)

Privatization and deregulation have been dominant symbols in economic policy across Europe in recent years. How far has the reality matched these symbols? Are we living in an era when the market is triumphant at the expense of state control of economic life? This book examines the analytical debates and the experience of a wide range of European countries, both east and west, including contributions from both lawyers and political scientists. Studies of the present state of privatization in the former Communist economies are matched by surveys of the state of deregulation in some of the most important capitalist states of western Europe. The authors emphasize the extent to which economic change is shaped by political strategies and interests, and the extent to which economic change has wide ranging constitutional implications.

This book will be essential reading for all those interested in making sense of the revolutionary changes now sweeping over the economies of the industrial world.

Contents
Introduction: politics, privatization and constitutions – Regulatory reform and privatization in Germany – Privatization and regulatory change: the case of Great Britain – Deregulation and privatization in Italy – Privatization and regulatory change: the case of Czechoslovakia – Privatization and regulatory change: the case of Poland – Environmental policy and regulatory change in Hungary – The political economy of ecological modernization: creating a regulated market for environmental quality – Conclusion: from national uniqueness to supra-national constitution – Index.

Contributions
Sabino Cassese, Michal du Vall, Kenneth Hanf, Jeremy Leaman, Tadeusz Markowski, Michael Mejstřik, Michael Moran, Istvan Pogany, Tony Prosser, Milan Sojka.

c.160pp   0 335 19072 3 (Paperback)   0 335 19073 1 (Hardback)

GOVERNMENT, INDUSTRY AND POLITICAL ECONOMY

Peter Barberis and Timothy May

The state of the economy has been the most important political issue in Britain for the last thirty years. Industrial performance plays a crucial part in determining the UK's economic fortunes. This book presents a detailed analysis of contemporary industrial policy in Britain. After an introduction on the nature of industrial policy, a number of different views about the role of the state in relation to industry and the economy are examined. A discussion of the major characteristics of the UK's industrial structure follows, concentrating on the most significant debates over the last fifteen years. The parts played by political parties and the major organized interests in developing various industrial policies are dissected. There is a detailed examination of major areas of contemporary industrial policy, including privatization, monopolies and mergers, regional policy, small business and local initiatives. The book concludes by posing the question 'could policy-makers have done better?'

The book draws together a wide range of material from official sources and academic analysis. It is written in a clear and accessible style and will be a key text for a variety of politics and economics courses.

Contents
Part I: The elements – The political economy of industrial policy – The anatomy of British industry – Britain's industrial decline: some explanations – The international dimension – Part II: The participants – Political parties – Employers and unions – The intelligentsia and informed opinion – Part III: Institutions and policies – Direction from the centre – Regional policy – Local industry: the regeneration of inner cities – Public ownership and privatization – Small business – Monopolies, mergers and competition policy – Conclusions – Appendix – Recommended reading – Bibliography – Index.

272pp   0 335 15680 0 (Paperback)   0 335 15681 9 (Hardback)

TOTAL QUALITY MANAGEMENT IN THE PUBLIC SECTOR

AN INTERNATIONAL PERSPECTIVE

Colin Morgan and Stephen Murgatroyd

TQM is a set of concepts, tools and applications which has been so successful in manufacturing industry that we are now witnessing experimentation in the transference of Total Quality Management to the public sector provision of government, health and education in North America, Europe and elsewhere. TQM is starting to set a new paradigm for management approaches in the public sector and 'not for profit' enterprises. All key public service managers will at least need to know the basics of TQM, its possibilities and limitations for the public sector, and particularly the types of applications which could work for them.

For all public sector managers this book provides: a clear understanding of the key concepts of TQM; a critical understanding of their fit and relevance to the public sector; empirical evidence of TQM applications in government, health and education; and exploration of the public sector TQM possibilities yet to be realized. It draws throughout on case examples from Britain, Canada, the USA and continental Europe which illustrate the application of TQM to the public sector.

Contents

Part 1: The nature of TQM in the public sector – Total Quality Management – Leading thinkers for Total Quality Management – Applying Total Quality Management in the public sector – Part 2: Applications of TQM to public sector organizations – TQM and health care – TQM and education – TQM and social services – TQM developments in government service – Issues and problems in adopting TQM in the public sector – Appendix – References – Index.

224pp   0 335 19102 9 (Paperback)   0 335 19103 7 (Hardback)

WHATEVER HAPPENED TO LOCAL GOVERNMENT

Allan Cochrane

In the 1980s British local government was at the eye of the political storm. Councils were blamed for overspending and central government was blamed for threatening to bring an end to local democracy. In 1990 a new local tax – the poll tax – proved so unpopular that it helped to bring an end to Margaret Thatcher's reign as Prime Minister. But what has really happened to local government over the last fifteen years? What do the changes tell us about the nature of British politics in the 1990s? And what do they mean for the future direction of local government?

These questions are at the heart of this book, which argues that it is necessary fundamentally to reappraise the ways in which we understand local government. Allan Cochrane develops a wide ranging argument, drawing on material from across the traditional divisions created by academic disciplines and theoretical systems to show that local government in Britain will never be the same again. It needs to be seen as just one element in a more complex local welfare state, which is itself being transformed to fit in with a new (business-led) agenda for welfare.

Contents
Introduction – Local government as welfare state – the 'end' of local government? – From state to market? – Towards the 'enabling' authority? – Post-Fordism and local government – Restructuring the local welfare state – From local government to local state: the impact of restructuring – References – Index.

160pp   0 335 19011 1 (Paperback)

IMPLEMENTING THATCHERITE POLICIES
AUDIT OF AN ERA

David Marsh and R.A.W. Rhodes (eds)

The politics and policies of the Conservative government under Prime Minister Margaret Thatcher constituted an undeniably distinctive phase in the history of post-war British politics. Her government claimed to have a radical policy agenda and placed a great deal of emphasis on achieving their objectives. This book examines the true extent of policy change in the 1980s, forsaking the conventional personalities and party rhetoric to focus on the hard question of 'What changed, by how much and why?' It compares the degree of policy change over a range of areas and explains why the extent of change was greater in some areas than others. The areas studied include: economic policy, industrial relations, local government finance, housing, social security, health, environment, agriculture and the European Community. The authors unearth a record of policy failure rather than transformation and argue that this failure was due to a lack of attention to implementation.

This important book will be of interest to policy makers, students and lecturers in social policy, politics, public administration and political economy.

Contents
'Thatcherism': an implementation perspective – Economic policy – Industrial relations – Local government finance – Housing – Social security – The National Health Service – Environmental policy – CAP and agricultural policy – The European Community – The implementation gap: explaining policy change and continuity – References and bibliography – Name index – Subject index.

Contributors
Jonathan Bradshaw, Peter M. Jackson, Peter Kemp, David Marsh, John Peterson, R.A.W. Rhodes, David Samways, Martin J. Smith, Hugh Ward, Gerald Wistow.

224pp   0 335 15682 7 (Paperback)   0 335 15683 5 (Hardback)

WHEN CITIZENS COMPLAIN
REFORMING JUSTICE AND ADMINISTRATION

Norman Lewis and Patrick Birkinshaw

This book sets out an agenda for reform of the institutions and practices through which citizens seek to achieve justice against public bureaucracies. The age of privatization has not removed from government the responsibility to ensure that social regulation, social welfare and provision of essential services are performed and/or provided in an equitable, efficient and responsive manner. The Government has acknowledged this responsibility in promoting and emphasizing the central position of the Citizens' Charter. The authors argue that there are certain duties which the state cannot evade and one of the most important of these is the provision of justice systems which allow citizens' voices to be heard and effectively responded to when the actions of governors or regulators adversely affect their interests. Efficiency and effectiveness have become bywords in the provision of services to the public; but how do these goals relate to justice and fairness? The authors examine overseas examples to see what useful lessons may be learned in the oversight and delivery of a just administrative system and how various methods for raising and resolving complaints may be enhanced and more effectively coordinated.

Contents
Justice against the state – The redress of grievances – Access to justice and the quality of administration – The supervision of justice – Optimum forms of dispute resolution – Tribunals and public hearings – The ombudsmen – Mechanisms operating within government organizations – Regulating utilities and self-regulation – The courts – Conclusion – References – Index.

240pp   0 335 15744 0 (Paperback)   0 335 15745 9 (Hardback)

Learning Resources
Centre